Intern Talk

A Guide to Walking the Walk

ANTHONY LOUIS

For permission and more information contact:

New Idea Press
A City of Light Publishing Imprint

2495 Main Street,
Buffalo, New York 14222

www.CityofLightPublishing.com

Book design by Ana Cristina Ochoa

ISBN: 978-1-942483-26-7 (softcover)
ISBN: 978-1-942483-19-9 (hardcover)

Library of Congress control number available upon request.

Printed in the U.S.A.

10 9 8 7 6 5 4 3 2 1

An internship is a rite of passage. In some cases, interns become full-time professionals at the companies where they served their internships. I don't need to stress how valuable these opportunities truly are in your journey, but in this book, I do aim to provide you with the ingredients and recipes needed to cook up successful, professional experiences. *Intern Talk* is a reference guide that not only focuses on how to secure an internship opportunity but also offers novel insights into securing a lifetime of career success.

— Anthony Louis

CONTENTS

INTRODUCTION

I began building the foundations of my career in high school. As soon as I recognized my interest in business, I began cultivating it. I started to read independently, book after book, biography after biography, and *Wall Street Journal* article after *Wall Street Journal* article. I absorbed the world of stocks and finance. I familiarized myself with prominent names and companies. I joined several organizations and clubs, which led me to join even more organizations and clubs. I attended dozens of networking events, workshops, and lectures. I studied, listened, learned, and then connected, expanding the scope of my interests and expertise tremendously. In fact, I still maintain and utilize some of the connections that I made years before entering college.

It is important when looking to become successful that you make an effort every day to seek out organizations and people outside the walls of academia who share the same budding interests. I'm sorry to tell you, though, that there's no secret formula to success. Where you start is simply where you finish. *You* are responsible for cultivating your interests by consistently seeking out knowledge, advice, and mentorship. This should be easy in the Information Age. The only thing that makes it hard is apathy. Being lethargic or cynical are surefire ways to prevent career success.

I won't lie. It's hard in the beginning when you are seeking out an appropriate internship. You'll send dozens of e-mails and get no responses. Why is that? Well, a significant number of internship seekers are rejected outright because of poor e-mail etiquette, underdeveloped résumés, and a lack of connections. But don't give up after a few rejections. Keep working and revising your strategies. Stay faithful to your beliefs and those uncertainties will morph into opportunities. You may not get it on the first try—I updated my résumé countless times. Eventually the effort you put forth will pay off.

I can honestly tell you that what helped me to mature into the young professional I am today are my faith and determination. I had faith in the advice I received from seasoned professionals. I had faith in the books I'd absorbed and the people I'd surrounded myself with. I was determined to find opportunities and grow professionally. If you have faith in yourself and determination in your work, you'll be able to avoid putting success on a pedestal out of reach. You must also understand that success is not defined by a single moment but is instead a process that turns into a routine if practiced every day. You can, and *should*, succeed every day, and the intent of this book is to help you learn how to do just that.

1

TALES FROM THE OFFICE

"At any moment, the decision you make can change the course of your life forever."

-Tony Robbins

As cliché as it might sound, by turning self-improvement and empowerment into a school of their own, you will discover more opportunities than you can possibly imagine. Here is my story of turning a bad experience into an opportunity for growth:

The Rubber Band Proverb

During my sophomore year of college I found out that I had been put on academic probation. To be honest, I had been doing poorly for a while. But I guess it took two semesters to realize that I was basically flunking out of school.

So there I sat, leaning back in my desk chair in deep reflection.

Eventually, a bag of rubber bands on my desk caught my attention. I needed to escape my racing thoughts. I was mentally exhausted. I wasn't in the mood to write, watch television, or do much of anything. I grabbed the rubber bands, popping one after another, back and forth. After a few hours, I was nearly out of rubber bands. Then one brought me back to reality. It didn't pop as easily as the others. My focus sharpened as I began to exert more effort. No matter how hard I tried, it simply refused to break. Intrigued, I began to examine the rubber band. I noticed it was different than the others. This one was made of a different material; it was a little thicker than the others. I gave it one more stretch, and as it finally popped, I had an epiphany.

Just like those many rubber bands, all of us are stretched, pulled, and twisted by life. Our personal problems, issues, fears, doubts, and experiences stretch us to the limit. And, like rubber bands, we must be elastic enough to endure the strenuous hardships of life. Some people are stretched until they can't take it—and they snap. This is what differentiates people in life: some are victims of circumstance and they allow themselves to be stretched until they are rendered fragile and useless. Just like you, the rubber band's ability to hold things together depends on the process by which it was developed. I decided then and there that I would not allow myself to snap. By making personal development and growth a lifestyle rather than a goal, I felt able to endure anything.

Who can stretch without breaking? They are the people who have mastered themselves and the world around them. They are the people who, while not complacent, are nonetheless patient with the universe. They embrace failure and welcome change as an opportunity to grow, regardless of the circumstances.

My goal in writing this book is not only to give you practical career advice, but also to provide you with the perspective necessary to understand and absorb these ideas. By the end of this book, you will understand how to stretch without breaking.

Jacob Couldn't Find a Job

I often meet with students to help them with their résumés and cover letters, as well as to offer career consultation. One particular student—we'll call him Jacob—came to me because he couldn't find a job.

The first thing I asked was how he was searching for opportunities. He seemed to be doing all the right things: using online sources, going to the career services center on campus, and attending career fairs. He was looking for an entry-level position that would help him get his feet wet in the finance industry. I asked him what he was doing to market and develop his professional brand. I also asked him what he was doing outside of college that would help attract employers. You see, Jacob, like many of the millions of college students and graduates seeking experience and full-time opportunities, was not maximizing his brand, which is the best way to get your foot in the door and attract opportunities (see Chapter Four: Personal Branding).

In today's workforce, recruiters assess a candidate's personal brand and online presence as much as they do his or her résumé. This means that conventional job-seeking just doesn't cut it anymore. In a sharing economy, the best way to find opportunities is through relationships.

What is a *sharing economy*? It's an economy that hosts more C2S (Consumer-to-Sales) relationships than B2B (Business-to-Business) relationships. Why do you think ventures and businesses like Uber and Airbnb are popping up? Crowd-funding vehicles and UX (user experience) technology are here to stay. We are not only eliminating the middleman, we are moving toward an economy in which the value of creativity and personal experience trumps all. We, the general public, are becoming the employers. Long ago, businesses focused on developing the best services. Now they're focused on developing the best experiences. How do they plan to do that? By developing their professional brand and marketing it to consumers.

You yourself are the business that is your brand. Sounds cheesy—and maybe it is—but it's also the truth. The businesses that fail today are those that do not know how to market themselves, regardless of how good their products are.

What I like about college, assuming you're entering university at a traditional age, is that it teaches you how to think. College forces you to organize your thoughts, your schedule, and your responsibilities in what is essentially a microcosm of 'real life.' You're forced to prioritize friends, parties, and the like. Maintaining a balance between social and academic life is probably the hardest thing college students face—and that doesn't change much immediately after collegiate life.

What's even worse than that is hearing them say, "I'm done with college! No more textbooks, tests, or books; it's time to work and make money!" Too many students stop developing themselves after college. They believe that all they need to succeed has already been given to them over the previous four years, but this idea is nothing but a farce.

I am not bashing college. I believe that a four-year degree is necessary for lots of types of opportunities. However, you must also understand that if you haven't been working in your career field, and if you haven't spent time connecting with alumni and professionals, you won't realize the single most important thing everyone needs to do in college: make your personal and professional development a priority. I ask you: What initiatives are you taking outside of the classroom? Are you doing enough independent reading and learning? All of that is part of your brand and being able to demonstrate that to professionals and employers is essential.

Jacob came to me for advice after months of searching for a job. He had been doing all the right things, but the economy and job market have changed in recent years. "All the right things"—all the things our parents and teachers were taught to do to get a job—are simply no longer enough. Together, Jacob and I revamped his strategy. We put together a list of a few networking events and conferences to attend over the following three months. He also started a blog that gave investing advice to college students, which in turn forced him to read more about investing and finances.

After a year or so, Jacob called with great news. At one of the conferences he attended he met two people who shared his interests. One was a financial advisor and the other was an investment banker. Jacob and the two other professionals used their skills and passion for the markets to found a financial startup, where he worked for about a year. Jacob then received a message on LinkedIn from the managing director of a big investment bank asking him about the startup he helped create. The director offered him the position of vice president at the firm.

"I was going about it all wrong," he told me. "All that time, I was chasing a job when I should have been chasing a better me." Jacob hit the nail on the head! Are you chasing titles and money, or are you focused on the real prize: personal development?

Jacob learned a lot by meeting new people and venturing out on his own. The lessons he learned by starting a company and managing a blog gave him the skills and experience necessary to become an extremely attractive candidate. By focusing on experiences that will better you and your brand, you will inevitably run into amazing opportunities. Your résumé alone could get you a job thirty years ago, but times are different. We live in an era in which people care about whom and what you know, which can't be accurately represented on a single sheet of paper.

I'm not saying that Jacob didn't struggle with his startup and his blog. He did, but he was failing forward. When he spent his time online "looking for a job" versus "looking for an experience," he wasn't moving forward at all. Jacob's personal projects humbled him and made him comfortable with failure. These experiences stretched his limits and allowed him to grow and strengthen himself. He did not snap, as did so many of those ill-fated rubber bands from my sophomore year of college.

Like Jacob, many students make the mistake of trying to build their résumés before trying to build themselves, which may land them an interview but will not give them the skills necessary to succeed in the long-term. Unlike companies and plans, people are allowed to fail; in fact, it was Jacob's 'failure' that allowed him to accomplish so much. In reality, the only time we really fail is when we fail to learn from our experiences.

The Law of Attraction

The Law of Attraction interprets the universe as a kind of living being that responds to positive and negative energy. The energy you emit finds a way to return to you. The idea of being a beacon of positivity and optimism is becoming very popular in the working world—even more so than in social realms. Remaining positive is a great asset to have, because throughout your life, many people will try to test your patience, character and values. Understanding how the Law of Attraction works will help you learn how to master yourself and, in doing so, how to deal with such people without causing harm to others or to the business.

My friend—let's call him Steven—is a perfect example of the Law of Attraction in action. When I first met him, he was always complaining about the things that were going wrong in his life, such as missed internship opportunities and other small misfortunes. I told Steven about the Law of Attraction and pointed out that the reason he wasn't enjoying life was because he was choosing not to. About a month later, I met Steven for drinks at a bar. Surprisingly, I did not meet the Steven I thought I knew. I met someone who was noticeably different; someone who was truly enlightened. He told me that he had finally started to understand that, although it is not possible to control everything that happens to you, you do have full control over how you respond to the universe and how you redirect your energy.

Life isn't perfect. You're going to be dealt a bad hand some of the time. But know that everything happens for a reason, and accepting the reality of the present is the start of a new beginning. "Life" and "reality" are two different concepts. Reality is what is true and what you cannot change. Losing your job is reality. Losing a loved one is reality. Performing poorly in school or failing a class is reality.

Life, on the other hand, is something much more personal and conscious. Life is the reality you create for yourself. It is contingent upon two things: the positive and negative energy you choose to emit in the world, and how you choose to think about the things that happen to you. There are some people with nothing in this world who are nonetheless happy and successful because they *choose* to be, regardless of their circumstances. These people do not blame the universe for any misfortunes they experience; they accept reality as it is, but they choose to alter how they *think* about life. While they aren't necessarily happy one-hundred percent of the time, when something bad happens to them, they're better equipped to deal with it and bounce back.

What ultimately bars you from remaining happy and living life is your ego—the voice inside your head that says everything will not be okay; that nothing is your fault and you are a victim of circumstance; that you cannot find happiness; that you won't get that internship, find that job, get into your dream school, or marry the perfect person. It is the voice of worry, guilt, blame, depression, arrogance, cockiness, and ignorance—and all that is negative. When did feeling sorry for yourself ever help you? When did asking the universe "Why me?" or "Why today?" help you? When did blaming someone else make your life any better? I'm not saying that you can't get mad, angry, or disappointed. We are all only human, and these feelings are part of our nature. At the same time, such negative, intrusive feelings only serve to stretch and twist you so that you eventually snap under mounting pressure. If you haven't already experienced this, you will as you mature and move further into your career. Instead of dwelling on the negative, learn how to use those emotions and frustrations as fuel for positive action.

Your early twenties will undoubtedly be one of the most confusing times of your life. Chances are you're going to feel like you don't have an exact hold on things. If so, you're not alone. Most students stress themselves out about what they want to do for the rest of their lives. Moreover, many aren't disciplined enough to concentrate on what they want; instead, they listen to what friends and parents tell them to want. Do what *you* want to do, not what other people tell you is the right thing to do. Focus on developing your skills and building a robust network and good things will come to you. Remember: staying positive in the present is the only way to stay in control of your own reality!

2

GETTING YOUR FOOT IN THE DOOR

"Opportunities are not found, they are made."

– Anonymous

Searching for and applying to internships is similar to applying to colleges for the first time. I know you remember how much time and effort you invested in that process: searching dozens of schools that fit your interests and needs, gathering letters of recommendation, and revising your personal statement over and over again. Now imagine how stressful your experience would have been had you waited until two weeks before the application deadline.

Internships have application deadlines too, and if you don't prepare your application well in advance, you're not going to have enough time to get everything done. Most students are rejected because they aimlessly hammer away at applications without any real preparation. This simply doesn't work! Internships aren't first-come, first-served. You need to take your time. There's no magic formula for an application that's absolutely guaranteed to get a response, but there are certain steps you should take, as well as things you should avoid at all costs.

Step by Step

Invest in the opportunity

This is crucial. To put it simply, the only way to increase your chances of landing an internship is by investing time searching for internships and carefully preparing your application. You'd be surprised at how many students complain that they have nothing to do over the summer and yet spent twenty minutes pressing "submit" on a billion online applications without researching the company or finding out whether they are the right fit for the job.

Expecting to get an internship that way is a waste of time. Instead, take your time networking. Don't stop asking professors, peers, friends and professionals for their advice and resources. Attend workshops on campus, networking events, and, of course, career fairs. Don't give up after searching and not finding anything, and don't wait until the last minute. You should be looking for opportunities around the clock, because the moment you stop looking is the moment you lose a potential opportunity.

Narrow it down

Dozens of internships will look interesting, but there is simply not enough time to apply to all of them. Instead, narrow it down to four or five opportunities—two or three if you have more experience. This will increase your chances, because you will be able to focus on tailoring each application to match exactly what the company is looking for. Employers are searching for the ideal candidate. They aren't in the business of hiring, they're in the business of business. If there's a spot open, they're looking for the one person who fits the description the best. Imagine Warren Buffet, one of the richest people in the world, applying to a bank teller job at your local Chase branch. He wouldn't get the job because he is obviously overqualified and therefore not the right fit. It's that simple.

Search for people who already work at the company

This is vital. After you narrow down your choices, seek out people who already work or have previously worked at the companies you are applying to. It's a good idea to find alumni from your school and ask them about what the employers are looking for in candidates. If you want to be sure they are willing to help, ask them first how they feel about students or recent graduates approaching them. It is natural to be a bit wary or nervous about approaching alumni—it was weird for me at first, too. But connecting with alumni will open more doors for you than you can imagine. They're not strangers, they're graduates of your school. Go on LinkedIn to find alumni, visit your school's career services center or online network, and look for networking events that feature employers with alumni from your school.

Find out what employers are looking for in a résumé

It's true that different industries and professions view résumés differently. Do some digging to see what recruiters in your field are looking for in candidates. These are the kind of things you should ask about at career fairs and networking events. Ask your professors, too. Even better, ask an employer directly when you get in touch with him or her.

Prepare your application and ready your resources

While you're doing research and networking, work on preparing your application. Be sure to get at least one letter of recommendation—more if possible, since they're a very valuable tool. When I'm applying for an opportunity, I challenge myself to include more credentials than asked for. This is what I call *supplemental material:* extra documents or materials added to your application which further demonstrate your qualifications as a candidate. Caution: *Don't do this if the application instructions specifically prohibit it or strictly limit the application components.* Think of anything you've written, designed, or created that will enhance your application. Make sure it's relevant and only include one to three examples of your absolute best work.

For example, when I was applying for a consulting internship, I included a business plan I wrote for an entrepreneurship class as part of my online application. Remember, they're looking for the ideal candidate, so it will increase your chances of landing the job if you can show them work you've done that's directly related to the position or the field.

Your application should include:

- A tailored résumé.

- A short cover letter or personal statement.

- At least one letter of recommendation.

- Additional/supplemental material relevant to the position.

Here are some tips on preparing each of these vital components:

Your Résumé

When recruiters look at your résumé, they'll spend thirty seconds skimming through your skills, experience, and education. If they find that your résumé is inconsistent with the job description, it will go directly into the trash. That is why it's important to focus on the few opportunities that you're really interested in.

Look at your résumé thoroughly and then read the job description and qualifications. Refer to them many times when tailoring your résumé and read your résumé as a recruiter would. Ask yourself: Does my résumé really reflect what the employer is looking for? What in my résumé would hurt my chances? What would help? Emphasize the stellar and remove the irrelevant. Read articles about the industry you're interested in and start to get a fundamental understanding of it. Networking with professionals already in that industry will also help you decide how to properly and precisely tailor your résumé.

Formatting

There is really no universally correct format for every résumé. The look and feel of résumés differs vastly across positions and industries. However, it is essential that your résumé be formatted in a way that allows you to fit the most relevant information on a single page. Recruiters should be able to easily navigate through your résumé. Don't suffocate them. They're just as interested in how your résumé is written and formatted as they are in what is in it. If your résumé appears disorganized or inconsistent, you will come across as disorganized and inconsistent. It doesn't matter what you have on it at that point. You're finished. The easier your résumé is to read, the better your chances are that it will be read. If you have a lot of experience on your résumé, consider breaking it up into categories (e.g. leadership experience, professional experience, etc.). Consider separating each section with fine lines. Hold your résumé at arm's length from people and ask them if it looks like something they'd want to read. If the answer is no, revise your format.

Always send your résumé as a PDF. Recruiters and professionals have told me this repeatedly. It's something that is very easy to forget, but it means a great deal because the formatting remains in place regardless of the device and operating system used to open it. If you create a beautiful résumé on your computer and then send it to someone who uses a different system, it can easily become unreadable, inaccessible or just plain jumbled. The fonts can change, bullets can move around, and your one-page résumé might turn into two pages with very little content on the second page, which looks sloppy. By converting your résumé into a PDF, anyone who opens it will see it just as you created it.

What to Put on Your Résumé

Recruiters want to know what you're learning both inside and outside of the classroom. Consider including the following information in the Education section:

Additional Coursework: Any courses or topics you took in school that are relevant to the position. Think long and hard. Perhaps you're applying to an accounting internship but do not have any direct experience in accounting. Add a course that you're taking or have taken relevant to accounting.

Core Competencies: Core competencies, also known as the "Skills" or "Qualifications" section, touch upon topics you gained an understanding of through direct experience. For instance, if you've done a lot of work in retail, you could list sales as core competencies. Perhaps you've learned a lot about stocks and finance through independent reading—include them as competencies. Remember to keep your audience in mind: What core competencies are recruiters looking for in your résumé? Core competencies are also an excellent way to add important words and key phrases that will help it pass the automated tracking system used by many employers to expedite the hiring process. If the right keywords are not in your résumé, you're not even going to make it to round one.

Technical Skills: These are any computer-based or application-based skills that you have like Microsoft Office, Aspen, HTML, Java, or Photoshop. Don't list all the technical skills that you have knowledge of; list the programming languages and software that you are truly competent using. Similarly, don't list skills that just about everyone has—most people know how to surf the internet, so you may not want to include 'internet browsing' as a skill.

Certifications and Licensures: Any official licenses or certifications that are current and relevant to the opportunity you're applying for, like Series 7, CPR, or CPA.

Always Tailor Your Experiences

I always tailor my résumé specifically to the position and company I am applying for. It is important that you use the position descriptions and qualifications listed on the company's website or on the actual application as the basis for writing your bulleted descriptions. If the online ad reads, "Looking for candidates with experience using logical reasoning and operational analysis," think of experiences where you had to use a similar array of skills and include them—and *only* them—in your résumé. Any irrelevant information will only hurt your application. Make sure to revisit the qualifications summary, several times if necessary. I actually keep the page open in front of me as I edit my résumé.

Writing the Bulleted Descriptions

Always use action phrases in your bulleted descriptions. Don't just give them a laundry list of responsibilities. Get in the habit of using descriptors like enhanced, increased, cut costs, and reduced. Recruiters want to see how you improved or at least contributed to your work environment. Use numbers or percentages whenever possible. If you created a presentation or collaborated on something, mention where or who it went to, and why. How many people worked on it? How did your project positively impact your work environment? Did it help cut costs, allow people to learn, or increase productivity? Trust me, it did something. Your job is to figure out what. Ask your manager, colleagues, and even clients if necessary. Focus on results!

Which of the two bulleted descriptions below do you find more impressive?

- *Used Microsoft Word to design templates for the marketing team*, or

- *Increased strategic opportunity by designing five advertising templates for the marketing team.*

Your accomplishments remain the same, but how you choose to describe them makes a significant difference in how they are interpreted. Don't sell yourself short! However, be careful not to exaggerate an experience that is relatively minor. Be specific and concise. Reduce your bullet points to one sentence whenever possible and always evaluate them for relevancy to the opportunity. Can they stand alone? Would this one point potentially move the résumé up on the employer's list? If not, it will only move it down—there aren't any neutral bullet points.

Turning Experiences into Experience

Students often lack real–world working experience but have many relevant experiences that compensate for this. Employers understand that students are still in school and are working to build their professional experiences. If it's an unconventional experience—perhaps you helped organize an event on campus, participated in a group project, or were heavily involved in the community outside of school—be sure to identify what you learned and the skills you used. Many students crop experiences out of their résumés either because they don't see the value in them or because they don't know how to effectively translate them into résumé-worthy experiences.

"But all I did was write a research paper. How do I add that to my résumé?" First, you had to use some set of skills to write the research paper. It had to be about something, and it had to have some kind of impact. Then it's simple: create a title for yourself and include the research paper name, a date range, and bullet descriptions.

Here are a baker's dozen of tips to make your résumé as robust and appealing as possible:

1. Don't include your high school education or experiences unless you are in your first year of college or you believe it is a résumé-worthy experience.

2. Include only one permanent address. Do not list your college address if you've already provided your home address, and vice versa.

3. Your statement of objective—if it's appropriate to use in your field—should be focused on what you hope you can do for the company, not want you hope to gain from the company in order to enhance your skills.

4. Include a URL to your LinkedIn profile. Employers are going to search for it anyway.

5. Avoid headers and footers. The information there get often gets jumbled or lost after going through the automated tracking-systems.

6. Categorize your Experience section. It helps employers scan your résumé more easily.

7. Always use "action phrases" in your bullet points (i.e., increased, reduced, added value, cut costs, improved, saved).

8. Always add statistics and figures that quantify your achievements. (i.e., "co-wrote a Loss Prevention Policy that reduced profit losses by three percent").

9. Organize your bullet points in descending order, starting with the most impressive and relevant.

10. Check for consistency. Make sure you use the same bullets, lines, and/or symbols and formatting throughout your résumé.

11. Exclude "References upon request." You should already be planning to provide letters of recommendation. Use professional references. Employers don't expect your friends and relatives to provide negative feedback about you.

12. Do not add any colors, graphics, or symbols that will take the reader's attention away from the content. Fancy résumés look goofy next to everyone else's standard black-and-white versions unless you're in a creative field.

13. Your résumé should be ONE page. Always!

Personal Statements and Cover Letters

Your cover letter, or personal statement, should not mimic your résumé but instead complement it. Don't write an essay summarizing all your professional experiences. There are two things you want to make sure you sell to the potential employer in your cover letter:

- You understand the position and what it takes to excel in it, and

- You're *personally* interested, motivated and qualified.

The first few lines should formally introduce who you are and identify the position and company you're applying to. Here's a quick example:

Greetings, Ms. Employer:

My name is John Doe, a senior finance student at Blank University. I am writing to formally express my interest in the Summer Analyst position at Company LLC.

Be sure to mention anyone with whom you've spoken who works at the company, as it may help your application make it to the "short stack." After your introduction, express your understanding of the position as well as why you're qualified for it:

I understand your company is seeking candidates with experience in finance, as well as the ability to build relationships and add value to Company LLC. My sincere interest in banking, coupled with a myriad of professional experiences that demand the use of financial analysis and planning, has instilled in me a baseline understanding of finance.

In the following example, I start with a strong opening by reciting the skills necessary for the job and explaining how I am professionally qualified:

I've been able to make connections between what I watch and what I read about market trends and the financial economy as I apply them in my professional experiences. Programs like Bloomberg News, Squawk Box, and books by prominent industry leaders have helped me find an intellectual home in the financial industry and outside of academia. Ultimately, I believe I have gained the quantitative thinking and logical reasoning skills necessary to succeed at Company LLC.

I included personal interests that are relevant to the position. Notice how I was able to express my sincere understanding of the Summer Analyst position by including the core skills relevant to the position (logical reasoning and quantitative thinking). I also show that I'm personally motivated because of the books I've read and the news I follow.

Finally, explain how a particular experience has prepared you for the position. If you're the treasurer of your fraternity, for example, express how that has prepared you for this opportunity:

I currently serve as the Finance Director of Beta Beta Beta on my campus. My student organization operates very much like a professional company. We organize meetings, hire and appoint officers, and ensure our success in the form of financial stability and professional development. This experience will allow me to naturally acclimate to the work environment at Company LLC. Serving as

Finance Director has taught me how to balance and interpret budgets and financial statements, invest in new opportunities, and remain solvent. I believe my personal and professional growth from this experience will enable me to significantly contribute to your company if accepted into your internship program.

I usually pinpoint the most relevant job experience in my résumé and then elaborate on it in my cover letter. Your cover letter should complement your résumé without rehashing it word-for-word. Always conclude your cover letter with a two-or-three-sentence paragraph that expresses your gratitude for the opportunity to apply and your contact information. My closing paragraph usually looks something like this:

> I'd like to thank you for your consideration and I hope to hear from you soon. Please feel free to contact me at xxxxx@xxx.com or 555-555-0000.

Your cover letter should be short and concise. I try to limit mine to about 300 words. This is your first formal contact with the employer, so you want to be personable yet professional. I sometimes go out of my way to mail the recruiter or hiring manager a signed cover letter, as well as attaching it to my online application. However, do *not* do this if the job listing specifically asks you to refrain from mailing or calling the company as that will knock you out of the running immediately for not following directions. Like writing a good résumé, writing a good cover letter requires skills that you will develop over time.

You should also ask professionals or friends to edit your cover letter. It's imperative that you get someone to read it, not just for content, but also for typos—which will ensure that your application gets thrown out immediately. Typos show an employer that you didn't take the time to proofread, implying that you are lazy. Even if you do proofread your own cover letter, you may still miss errors; because you know what you *meant* to write, your brain will view it as correct.

Letters of Recommendation

The most circulated fallacy about letters of recommendation is that you have to be of a certain age or status to write one. A letter of recommendation is simply an endorsement written by someone you have worked for or who can attest to your work ethic and character. It is recommended that you seek letters from older professionals, such as professors, bosses, and mentors, because they are thought to be more credible sources. However, I've written a few recommendations for peers, as well. If you have worked for and alongside friends as partners, members of the same student organization, or as an employee, it's fine to seek their endorsements if appropriate.

Still, I fully support seeking the endorsement of an older professional before going to a friend or peer. I believe that these letters are the second most important component of any application—your résumé being the first. These endorsements add credibility and value to your application when they are authored by individuals who have some level of authority and responsibility. Far too many students neglect letters of recommendation because they are not aware of how much of a difference they make. Always include a letter of recommendation when applying for any opportunity, especially if one is not required!

Now that you see how much work goes into these applications, think about how much time you'll need to complete them all. It's vital that you invest time in this activity because taking action and following these steps are the only ways to secure a number of great opportunities to choose from. A lot of other people are competing with you for these positions, so putting the work in when others don't will show that you are willing to put time and effort into the jobs you set your mind to. This is an important way of proving to potential employers before they even meet you that you are a hard worker.

It's not that difficult to land an internship or a job after college if you don't cut corners when you apply. Sure, it's competitive but it's not impossible if you're willing to invest time in the application process. The main reason many students miss out on great opportunities is because they fail to go the extra mile. Make sure you have done everything you can in packaging your application rather than just submitting your résumé and expecting to get an internship. That's just the bare minimum. After all, would you have applied to your college with just the online application— no personal statement, recommendation letters, or high school transcript? The companies you're applying to take the recruiting process seriously, especially if you're applying for a paid internship. They want to make sure their time and money are well spent.

So, You Got an Interview

Now what are you going to do with this valuable opportunity to make a great impression and close the deal? Here are some tips for acing an interview.

Most interviewers ask clichéd questions, such as "Why do you think you are a good fit for this company?" and "Tell me a time you had to overcome a challenge." They do this for a good reason: your answers will tell the interviewer a lot about you in a short amount of time. Your answers should allow them to envision you as a future colleague and not just a random applicant. You want to make them feel like they're participating in a conversation rather than an interview. The candidates who "ace" interviews are those who show employers that they know what they're talking about and answer questions thoughtfully and thoroughly. They're looking for people who are passionate, mature, and intelligent. Always stop and think about what you're going to say beforehand instead of blurting it out, even if you've prepared for the question. It shows employers that you take the time to think through problems long enough to come up with the best solution.

Preparation

I make a habit of reading several online articles before I go in for an interview. I search for interviewing tips and thoughts from CEOs, hiring managers, and industry experts on LinkedIn, Google, and other sources. Getting into the heads of these recruiters is a surefire way of making sure you are prepared, helping you to understand their thought processes and giving you the confidence to walk in ready to answer any and all questions to the best of your ability. Be sure to research common interview questions, strategies, and advice.

Do your homework on the company, as well. Find out what they are currently doing and why you would want to be a part of it. Try to locate alumni on LinkedIn who either are employed or were employed by the company you're interviewing with. Ask as much as you can about the interview process and compare what they say with what you read online.

Complete at least two practice interviews before the actual interview. This will help you isolate any potential weaknesses and build the confidence necessary to do well. Learn how to answer key questions the interviewer may ask and how to emphasize your strengths. The single most important product of these mock interviews is feedback. Feedback, feedback, feedback. Ask for as much of it as possible. You can't do your best if you don't know whether what you're doing is right or wrong. Don't just sit down with your best friend; it's important to meet with someone who is versed in interview strategies, who can point out what you're doing wrong and tell you how to fix it. You don't want someone who's never been interviewed to say, "Yeah, sure. Sounds good." Go to your career services center, sit down with a friend or mentor, and reach out to employers in your field. Record your mock interviews so you'll be able to see and hear yourself and iron out any "rough spots."

It's natural to be nervous during an important interview, but don't take it so seriously that you can't think. Be relaxed yet aware of your mannerisms. Now, I'm not here to sugarcoat things. If you're so nervous during an interview that you aren't able to keep your composure, then you simply aren't ready—and that's okay. You will build confidence and self-assurance the more you practice and interview with employers. You'll get there. I did.

Last-Minute Preparations

Arrive for the interview fifteen minutes early—no earlier, no later. This will provide time for any unexpected bumps in the road: traffic jams, getting lost, parking issues, etc. without stressing out and being late. Arriving early takes some pressure off and also gives you time to mentally prepare. When you arrive early to your interview, ask to use the restroom so you can do the following three things:

1. **Check your appearance.** Take a few minutes to make sure your wardrobe is in order: dress or suit looks clean, tie is straight, etc. Also make sure your teeth and face are clear of food and smudges.

2. **GET PUMPED.** Talk to yourself. Remind yourself why you're there as opposed to someone else. Remind yourself why you deserve this. Only POSITIVE thoughts! Leave the fear and doubt where they belong: out of sight.

3. **Actually use the bathroom.** Having to go during the interview will make you feel rushed and negatively impact your answers. Excusing yourself during the interview is not an option.

Take in Tangibles

Talking about your experiences is one thing, but bringing in, say, a copy of your personal fashion portfolio or a mock sales report you created for a class is evidence that backs up your claims of experience. This shows employers that you are able to take what you've learned in college and apply it in real life. Feel free to get creative but remain relevant. Also, be sure to bring a copy that you don't mind leaving behind. This gives them the opportunity to look it over while you're being considered and could make the difference between a hire and a rejection.

Selling Your Weaknesses

"What are some of your weaknesses?" is still a common interview question, but the "correct" answer has changed. Don't give them the "I work too hard" fluff that used to work ten years ago. Employers are tweaking their questions and paying closer attention to what your responses tell them about your confidence, self-awareness, and honesty. They're measuring your sense of integrity and humility. Employers know that you aren't perfect, but they want to see if *you* know that.

Still, this question is one of the trickier ones. There's a way to sell your response without turning off your interviewer. Directly telling your interviewer something like "I don't work well on teams" could be a deal-breaker. You have to be careful not to say anything that can be easily misinterpreted—it's all about *how* you articulate your answer.

The way I usually answer this question is by finding an obvious discrepancy between the job opportunity and my experiences—specifically something that is not a deal breaker. Say you meet most of the qualifications but there's one preferred skill that you are missing. Perhaps, they "prefer" someone with Excel and PowerPoint, but you only have PowerPoint. Explain that Excel isn't something you've had exposure to, but you are very much willing to learn. This is a great way to approach this kind of question because missing a preferred skill is something apparent (since it's not on your résumé) but will probably not disqualify you.

The Art of Storytelling

If you're in an interview, chances are your interviewer is going to ask you to tell them about a time when you've failed. Talking about your failures is difficult because it usually requires telling a story. The best way to articulate a failure is by turning it into a *successful failure*: an experience where you were unable to achieve the initial goal but still gained something positive in the process. The idea is for you to impress them with what you learned from your "failure," which will show them that you are positive and goal-oriented, not to mention mature enough to value your failed experiences.

Explaining a failure is easy. You do this by expressing:

- The skills you used to work towards the initial goal.

- Any positive realizations from that experience (an unexpected positive outcome, or something you learned from the experience).

- What you could have done differently to reach your initial goal.

Here's a story of one of my personal failures:

During the spring of my junior year of college, I organized a concert on campus to raise money for my student organization. I invited a few friends who were artists from New York City to perform and booked a lot of student poets. Guess what? Hardly anyone came. Of the two hundred to three hundred people who I expected to attend, only about thirty showed up. At first, the event seemed like a total flop, but the concert still went on, and during the performance, something magical happened. I translated my disappointment into positive energy and, in doing so, I realized that I had created something really cool. The few dozen people who attended couldn't stop talking about what a great time they had and that the opportunity to connect with other artists was worthwhile for them. Moreover, the smaller audience allowed for a more intimate setting—everyone was able to talk to one another. In short, my "failure" humbled me. Even though I lost the money I invested in the concert, I was able to look past my failed expectations and understand the positive impact it had produced. We all create great things, but sometimes it's hard to see your success when the outcome is different than anticipated. When you think that you failed, whether at your internship or at school, try to realize that it is just another opportunity to learn. After the concert, I wrote down everything I could have done differently, like advertising more aggressively, and I promised myself that I would reference the list the next time I planned an event.

Employers don't care that you failed at something, they just want to examine how you reflect on your decisions. Companies make large mistakes all the time, but they need people who think resiliently and who can help re-strategize in the face of failure or loss.

"So, Tell Me About Yourself" OR "What's Your Story?"

Your answer to this probe is one that can win over the interviewer. If answered properly, this question can give the interviewer everything they need to know to make an informed decision. But it can also be a death knell. It is critical to understand that employers want to know your professional story, not your personal life story. The real question they are asking is, "Why should we hire you?"

Start with your university and major—why did you choose them, what's the brief story behind those choices? Don't be afraid to personalize just a bit: "Before deciding to go to college, I contemplated military service." "Heading to university was advice given to me by a dear mentor of mine." "I chose to study political science because it was something I believed would provide me with a diverse outlook on relationships and community."

From your educational background, move through your experiences. Don't dwell too long on each experience—I suggest focusing on one or two things you've learned through each, and how that knowledge applies to the opportunity for which you're interviewing. Finally, bring your answer into the present. Reiterate your interest in the opportunity: this is basically your pitch. It is the question you need to practice answering the most during your mock interviews.

Questions Drive Conversation

Always ask questions at the end of the interview. This is a great time for you to impress the interviewer. I have *four key questions* that I try to always ask at the end of an interview.

What does success look like during the first thirty days? This shows that you are motivated and seek to do well in the position.

What has kept you here? Employers are always looking for forward-thinking individuals and this shows that you're thinking long term.

I'm really invested in personal and professional develop-ment. Could you recommend any good books? Employers want to see that you're a lifelong learner who continually invests in yourself.

Are there any concerns regarding my candidacy that you'd like me to address? This is the question I always ask last. It shows the employer that you're taking this opportunity seriously. Moreover, it shows them that you are very ambitious and self-aware; it tells them that you're always looking for ways to improve yourself, and consequently, the company you work for.

Even if the employer doesn't ask you if you have any questions, take the initiative at the end of the interview. This is one of the things that will make the interview feel more like a conversation and it will set you apart from other candidates. Be sure to first ask, "Do you mind if I ask a few questions?" Time constraints might lead you to limit yourself to just one or two of the above suggested questions to respect the interviewer's schedule.

Follow Up!

Always follow up within forty-eight hours of your interview. A short e-mail that simply expresses your gratitude and appreciation for the opportunity will suffice. Here's an example:

Hello Mr. Johnson,

I hope this e-mail finds you well. I'd like to express my gratitude for the time you spent speaking with me. I appreciate your consideration.

I look forward to hearing from you.

Thank you.
Best,

[Your name]

What If I Am Rejected?

Rejection, unfortunately, is a part of life. What's dangerous is that students' natural reflex is to blame themselves and assume that they aren't good enough. A lack of professional experience and skills might be to blame—everyone starts somewhere.

Do not let a rejection damage your confidence!

Instead, look at a rejection as an opportunity to further show your passion for the profession. Express your appreciation for the opportunity and note that you understand the decision. If possible, connect with the employer or recruiter on LinkedIn. They just might remember you next time an opportunity arises.

Then reflect appropriately and learn from the experience. Did you miss something in the application? Did you miss some keywords in your résumé or fail to tailor it correctly? How about the interview? Did you not practice enough or prepare the right things? Did you familiarize yourself sufficiently with the industry?

Ask yourself objective questions but do not doubt your confidence or character. Everyone makes mistakes, but successful people learn from them. Moreover, all of that hard work will not go to waste. Understand what you could have done better and apply it to your next interview.

You're Hired!
Your First Day on the Job

Your first day will be either very slow or very busy, depending on different factors. Usually, however, it's very slow. You're probably going to spend time completing paperwork, setting up your computer, and meeting your colleagues and supervisors. Use this first day to hit the ground running!

Ask your supervisors for any reports, company literature, department reference guides, contact sheets, floor plans of the office, or anything else they think you might need. I remember asking an associate at one job if she had any instructions on how to use the company's internal online system. Not only did she provide me with one, she also gave me a sheet that listed dozens of inter-office acronyms that I needed to know as well as other useful literature. It took me ten seconds to ask the question but having those documents at my disposal saved me dozens of hours of learning and prevented many mistakes over the course of my internship.

Open communication is very important, especially on the first day, so be sure to make clear your willingness to jump in. Open up your networking avenues and become comfortable with the work environment.

The lifeblood of an intern is the ability to network. Try not to grab lunch by yourself the first day; take someone out to lunch or grab a group lunch with coworkers or fellow interns. Make sure you let your supervisor know that you are interested in meeting as many people as possible. This will not only illustrate enthusiasm, but it will also help your supervisor keep you in mind when he or she meets with new people. It may seem intimidating at first, but you'll be happy you asked!

Set Personal Goals

Not everyone thinks to do this, but you need to establish personal goals, especially if there aren't really any formal goals set for you. Showing your manager that you have a plan to better yourself indicates that you are passionate and engaged, goal-oriented and focused. If you're going to work hard to better yourself, it will be clear to your supervisor that you will probably work hard to better the company, as well. Avoid setting unrealistically lofty goals; instead take large goals and break them down into weekly or daily accomplishments—also known as KPIs (Key Performance Indicators).

Be Proactive, Not Reactive

Ask every question that comes to mind. You can only get answers by asking questions. The worst thing you can ever hear at work is "Why didn't you ask?"

After years of internship experiences, I can attest to the fact that there is indeed no such thing as a stupid question. Asking as many questions as possible shows that you are engaged and motivated. A surprising number of people are too worried about looking foolish to speak up. Instead, they try to figure everything out on their own, inevitably making at least one mistake that could have been avoided. Asking questions makes you look smarter, not dumber, so ask as many as you need. However, don't just make up questions that you already know the answer to in order to convince your manager that you're making an effort. That will just get you a reputation for wasting people's time—also, try not to ask something that you could perhaps Google yourself.

You will undoubtedly make mistakes, and sometimes supervisors won't mention your mistakes directly to you but instead make mental notes of them. Be sure to make it clear that you know you are going to make mistakes and that you welcome all feedback. And most importantly, learn from the feedback you receive no matter who provides it.

Finally, you should always be working on something. When things are slow, try to find work or create a project for yourself. If you're not sure what to do, ask your supervisor to assign you a task. Taking the initiative is something that should be recognized in every workplace. Never wait for anyone to give you work. Instead, find daily ways to contribute to your work environment. Work on refining things like attention to detail, communication, and time management. Meet regularly with your supervisor to keep track of your progress.

Once you have the internship, these are ways that you can help increase the odds that your supervisor will either hire you after it's completed, or provide you with good references or a letter of recommendation for future job applications.

What If I Don't Like My Internship?

Working at a job or internship that you don't like is never fun, but it's important to see it through. I've had too many conversations with interns who did not put in 120 percent simply because they didn't like their position or believed they weren't growing and learning. What you get out of your internship is about how your frame your experiences. You may not like the work or the people you work with, but that doesn't mean you're not growing or learning. Guess what? Chances are, you're probably not going to love your first job out of college either, but it is an opportunity nonetheless. Invest your time and energy because you appreciate the experience, and because the more you put into it, the more you will get out of it. If you don't, you will spend months not only doing something you don't like, but you will also have lost out on a chance to leave a strong impression that could help you get your foot in the door somewhere else.

Perhaps you've come to the realization that this is not the career path you'd like to follow ... so what? The core skills that you'll learn investing 100 percent in your internship are priceless: communication, attention to detail, professional writing, and much more. These are core skills that translate across just about any industry and profession.

3

TAKE THE "WORK" OUT OF NETWORKING

"My golden rule of networking is simple: don't keep score."

– Harvey Mackay

Networking is the exchange of information between individuals, groups, and institutions, specifically for the cultivation of productive relationships. So why do college students generally consider socializing and networking to be two very different things? It's because networking is often only considered necessary when seeking an internship or a job. As we mature, though, the dividing line between socializing and networking disappears, and these two crucial endeavors meld into one.

Understanding Networking as a Way of Life

As we develop our adult selves, we begin to make new friends and connect with people who we can succeed with and learn from. Professionals socialize and network simultaneously all the time at cocktail parties. Yep, that's right. As you get older, you'll learn how to network and drink *at the same time*. In this section, I'll show you how to take the "work" out of "networking" so it feels more natural.

Opportunities Are Made, Not Found

One time I was on the train heading to work when I saw a woman reading a book that she appeared to be very interested in; she kept nodding her head as she read. An avid reader myself, I asked her about the book. She was reading what has since become one of my favorite books: *The Seven Spiritual Laws of Success* by Deepak Chopra. Our conversation about the book led to a brief chat about success and what success means. She told me that I had a very bright future ahead of me and that we should definitely keep in touch. We exchanged business cards and connected on LinkedIn. Had I not taken the initiative to speak with her on the train, this relationship would not exist.

Always be aware of your surroundings and make networking a way of life. It's important to remember that you can pick and choose which conversations to participate in, and different settings bring with them different expectations. The atmosphere, of course, is more formal at interviews and professional networking events. In those settings, you're expected to talk about jobs, college, and careers. With a stranger you should still be professional and seek permission to ask questions that are more personal. For example: "If you don't mind my asking, how did you get started in that field?"

There are also times when you can be a bit more casual. Don't stress too much about who you are and what you aren't "supposed" to do when networking. Just use common sense and you'll be fine. For example: Should you wear a ball gown or flip-flops to a formal networking event? Obviously, the answer is no to both—business casual is the appropriate attire. When in doubt, ask someone who has attended the event before or the people organizing it. Should you tell the professional you're talking to that hilarious dirty joke your roommate told you last night? Absolutely not. But can you make a joke about the weather, traffic, or some other safe topic if the opportunity arises? Sure. This is all stuff you probably know intuitively or have already been told, so trust your instincts and you'll be fine.

If productivity and success are routinely at the forefront of your thoughts, you're definitely networking a lot of the time, and not just at networking events. If they aren't front of mind, you should work on keeping them there. In short, the key to becoming a great networker is to make it a personal and lifelong habit to seek new connections, engage in productive conversations, and cultivate relationships regardless of your environment. Remember to ask questions about the person you are talking to rather than focusing on your story and your needs.

By training your brain to think in terms of productivity, you're more likely to participate in fruitful conversations from which you can learn and benefit. Most networking doesn't require a suit and tie or a résumé, just the ability to engage in great conversations with ambitious people.

Why Network?

If you're at a networking event for the sole purpose of finding a job, then you are in the wrong place. Professionals and executives attend networking events to expand their networks. Why would they network if they're already well along in their careers? They go to exchange ideas and advice. I'm not saying you can't keep opportunities in mind, but your main focus at one of these events is not to find a job. Go in as an open book, ready to absorb the room and everyone in it. Unless it's an actual job fair, don't even mention anything about jobs. If you network effectively the opportunities will come to you.

At a networking event you're aiming to do one thing: inspire. Moving people to act with whatever they're doing in life is the essence of networking. By inspiring others and motivating people to be their very best, you'll be able to build countless valuable connections. Some of the greatest mistakes I see people make at networking events are selfishly seeking opportunities, admiration, and affirmation for themselves. They don't understand the difference between receiving feedback and stroking their ego. What is even more dangerous is that they generally don't understand that this is what they're doing. By focusing on themselves and not on other people, they are missing out in a substantial way.

The ability to motivate and inspire others is a characteristic found in great leaders. If you are viewed as an individual with inherent leadership skills, that reputation will take you farther than you can even imagine. This means that when you're networking, you should genuinely listen and pay attention to what people are saying about themselves. It is just as important to pay attention to the moods and body language of the people you interact with. If they doubt something about themselves or their goals, offer some affirmation and encouraging words. As Maya Angelou once said, "People may not remember what you did, or even what you said, but they will remember how you made them feel."

Networking in Action

Now that you have a firm grasp on the need to network, let's go over some aspects of networking that might be helpful in practice. Engaging people at professional networking events isn't very different than doing this at a friend's party. Just remember to be personable, professional and inquisitive.

Be Personable

Many college students feel the need to turn off their personalities at professional events. Don't do that. Instead, show your human side by engaging in conversations about childhood and personal goals with other professionals. Exchanging stories will help you build rapport and connect on a more personal level. Don't be one of the young professionals trying to break into the workforce by striking up conversations that revolve only around their résumé and potential opportunities. Employers and professionals receive e-mails and phone calls several times a week about kids looking for internships. It gets tiring.

Learning what people do outside of the workplace may tell you more about them than just their job title or accomplishments. Throw titles and corporate-speak out the door—everyone has a backstory. Being personable involves an exchange: share your ideas, ambitions, and fears. These personal exchanges will break down barriers and help the professional you're talking to remember you personally—and honestly, that's all that matters. I understand that you may be wary of getting too personal, but a good sense of professionalism can alleviate this stress.

Be Professional

Professionalism is something that is cultivated over time. It comes with maturity and emotional intelligence. People can "look" or "appear" professional—a dapper suit and strong vocabulary give that impression—but true professionalism is much more than that.

Respect is at the core of professionalism. This includes keeping track of how long you've talked to someone, apologizing if you feel like you've inadvertently insulted or wronged them, and asking before you take a seat or touch something. Try to avoid sensitive areas of discussion, but if you feel the need to broach a personal topic, be sure to request permission. *Always* take the initiative and ask. It shows that you are indeed professional. If the person you're talking to brings up something that you disagree with, refrain from expressing a position too strongly.

Be Inquisitive

Asking thoughtful and thought-provoking questions is the best way to show people that you appreciate their time and recognize their intellectual prowess. If you meet a marketing professional at your school's alumni event, for example, don't ask them if they studied marketing in college. Try instead to ask them if they were always creative growing up, or how marketing drives their everyday life. I like to call these *penetrating questions*, and they help lead the way to more stimulating conversations. More importantly, though, they help to differentiate between someone who is merely curious and someone who is intellectually inquisitive.

Understand that questions are what drive dialogue. Here are a few sample questions:

- *Are many in your family doctors, or are you the first to go into medicine?*

- *How does working with engineers every day shape the way you think?*

- *What are some of your personal interests outside of your career?*

- *What does it take to become a leader, especially in the [fill-in-the blank] industry? Are there specific characteristics you look for?"*

- *How can I differentiate myself from my peers who are seeking the same opportunities?*

One very important attribute that is difficult to define and even harder to cultivate is the ability to express passion. It helps to present yourself as a colleague rather than as a student and to think of penetrating questions to ask. To cultivate these questions, you must familiarize yourself with the latest trends in the industry. Read a few articles the day before the networking event. It's important that you offer your own opinions and ideas. This shows you're able to think for yourself and that you're not just another college student trapped in a bubble. Don't think of them as professionals, think of them as mature colleagues in suits.

Professional Networking

Professional networking takes place in environments or situations organized for the express purpose of exchanging conversation about mutual career or personal interests. Here are some tips:

What if you find yourself standing on the periphery of a networking event contemplating how to blend into the crowd without seeming obnoxious or interrupting someone? Start by choosing a subgroup. Look for the largest gap in the crowd and try to smile your way into a standing spot. If your chosen spot disturbs those speaking or listening, just quietly apologize and choose a different group. Stand close enough to the edge of a group to listen in on the discussion. This will allow you to tune in to details or ideas so that when you do jump in, you're prepared to add to the conversation.

Group networking is both good and bad. It's easier for shy types because it takes the attention and pressure off. Unfortunately, it's also easy for professionals to forget who you are if you're not actively mingling. You must be sure to make eye contact with everyone in the group while talking—the more eyes on you, the better. You want people to remember who you are. Always try to bounce off others' ideas and thoughts; it sends the message that you work well with others and can retain information.

Try to exchange business cards with everyone in the group, as well. This is not being pushy. Just as you would bring everyone something to drink if you had several guests over to your house, you show respect by exchanging your contact information with everyone in the group.

When you wish to migrate to another group, apologize for leaving the circle, and always share your thanks and appreciation before you exit. Take your leave during a pause—never while someone is speaking. If the group seems like it's still in full swing, I wouldn't recommend asking for people's information, since that would be an interruption. Make a mental note of who you were connecting with and go back to exchange business cards later during the event.

Follow Up

Do not fail to follow up on a networking session with e-mails. Business card by business card, thank each and every person whom you met for their time. Try to mention something you took away from the conversation—advice, a story, anything—and tell them you're looking forward to staying in touch.

Reverse Networking

Unless it was mentioned at the event, or the networking event was specifically organized for recruiting, avoid internship and job talk in your e-mails. Asking questions of this nature in the follow-up to a general networking opportunity will make you seem self-serving. Instead, offer your help and resources. This is known as *reverse networking*. By serving as a bridge to others, employers will see an honest candidate who is interested in bettering the people around them. For example:

Hi, Jane/John,

I hope this e-mail finds you well. It was a pleasure to meet you at the XYZ event. I enjoyed discussing writing and publishing with you, and it was interesting to learn that you have a book in the works. If you need any help marketing your book to students on my campus, I would love to share my contacts and resources with you.

I'm looking forward to keeping in touch. Thank you.

Connecting others to opportunities while networking, versus looking for opportunities for yourself, is very powerful because you not only gain new contacts but simultaneously nurture relationships with both new and existing connections. People naturally remember those who have helped them out.

I have enjoyed many opportunities because I invested time in serving as a bridge between different connections. My connections, in turn, made it a habit to return the favor by relaying invitations, scholarship opportunities, endorsements, etc. Reverse networking is also advantageous because it helps shape your image. Talk to as many people as possible, even professionals outside of your career interests. Again, people have lives outside of their professional careers and those lives include friends and family who come from many different walks of life. So what if you are an engineering major? Find out what Joe does at XYZ Bank. Who knows? His family might be full of engineers. This is one of the reasons that it is important to exchange stories about family and childhood. Life outside of college isn't compartmentalized into majors and schools. Lawyers network with bankers; bankers network with doctors; doctors network with politicians; and so on...

Networking on the Job

It's much easier to network on the job since you already have a relationship with co-workers. If you're at a sizable office, try stopping by cubicles to chat with coworkers or pick up lunch for someone who can't get away from his or her desk that day. Take the initiative and ask if anyone needs help with what they're working on. Or, if you notice something that needs attention, get the job done quickly and accurately and notify the appropriate person. Try not to step on anyone's toes, though. If it's something you downloaded or created yourself, feel free to jump right into it. If it's a file or project, be courteous and ask permission. If in doubt, always ask.

Be proactive. Ask a coworker to introduce you to someone you'd like to meet, or introduce yourself to that person. If possible, try coordinating events during your internship, like an intramural team sports. You can meet a lot of new people that way. Taking initiative makes people more likely to invite you to their events, in turn, where you will make even more connections.

Networking at work is about nurturing relationships. For example, on the last day of a summer internship, I brought in a red velvet cake for my team so that we could share our farewells and our best wishes together. Doing small things like this really shows you're invested in the organization and are looking to build and sustain relationships.

Water Cooler Conversations

Chances are your office has a water cooler in the lounge or kitchen area and, yes, you will engage in casual conversations with coworkers and supervisors there. You don't have to introduce yourself to every single person who crosses your path, but introducing yourself to new colleagues around the office is a vital part of networking.

This internal networking is no different than the other types of networking that we've talked about. Remember to be personable, professional and inquisitive. Keep the conversation reciprocal by taking turns exchanging questions and comments, and be sure to ask penetrating questions. Do not gossip. Since you are at work, you should check the time every now and again while you're in a conversation with someone and ask if you're holding them up, showing that you value their time and work schedule. Be sure to make a note of where the person sits, so you can follow up later.

Career Talks

A career talk is an informational interview: a meeting with a seasoned professional to discuss career interests. Treat these chats just as you would a conventional interview. Always bring a notepad, especially to a career talk; since you are seeking advice, taking notes is expected. However, do not allow note-taking to distract you from the conversation. Be subtle. Apologize if you feel like you've taken your attention away from the conversation for too long. Do not try to capture every word, just jot down the highlights. Make it a conversational habit to always reaffirm when you hear something noteworthy, which shows your engagement.

Practice Makes Perfect

Make it your responsibility to sit down with the person you report to whenever their schedule allows. These one-on-one conversations will not only help demonstrate your appreciation for the opportunity you have been given but also help establish a relationship with your supervisor and polish your networking skills. Make these meetings short and sweet and be sure they are productive. Remember the networking principles: *personable, professional*, and *inquisitive*. It's no different in your boss's office. Regularly exercising these networking principles at work will help you create a concrete networking strategy.

However, it's extremely important to note first what kind of person your supervisor is. If they are strictly business, you should only discuss how your work is going. If they seem more personable and interested in your life outside of the company, it's okay to ask for advice about school or other areas of life. Be careful not to treat your supervisor like a parent or a guidance counselor; you shouldn't be running to them with problems you have with professors, significant others, or roommates. Follow your supervisor's lead in determining what is and isn't appropriate to talk about.

The main thing you're looking for from regular talks is feedback. Outside of your actual work, you're trying to refine yourself as an individual. If it's appropriate, ask for advice about achieving personal aspirations, interests, and goals, as well as advice on networking, school, and life.

Getting the Most Out of Networking

Attend more networking events. Sounds simple, but you'd be surprised at how many students do not network enough—if at all. Not only should you be networking regularly outside of professional events in everyday life, you should be actively looking for different events to attend. Pay attention to the flyers and bulletin boards on campus. Attend career fairs, guest speaker events, and participate in programs offered by your campus. I know how it is sometimes. You think, "I don't feel like going by myself," or, "It's not a big deal. I'll go next time." But the more events you go to, the more chances you have to make connections. One job fair might be a bust, but the next one might lead to a great opportunity. Go to as many as you can and take full advantage of them! Go with a group of friends if it makes you feel more comfortable, but do not stand around and talk with them. That defeats the purpose!

Attend Conferences

These events provide a great deal of quality networking opportunities. Students typically shy away from conferences because they cost money. However, that should not stop you. Conferences are a prudent investment. I say "invest" in conferences because they are where people who are serious about their careers spend time discussing goals and industry trends, and, of course, networking. Many conferences offer discounts for college students, and offering to volunteer at a conference will often get you a complementary pass.

Join Organizations

If you're still in college, networking couldn't be easier. I don't think there is any other environment that provides such an abundance of networking opportunities. Your GPA is important—especially if you're gunning for a competitive program like nursing or engineering—but so is making connections outside of the classroom.

Look into joining at least one or two relevant organizations or clubs to serve as a networking hub. Universities and colleges generally have dozens if not hundreds of on-campus organizations that travel, host networking events, and provide scholarship opportunities. Surround yourself with current as well as future professionals. Offer to take on responsibilities in these groups: chair committees, coordinate events, perhaps even run for student office.

Before It's Too Late

You need to do this networking while you're still in school for the same reason most people are in college to begin with: to find a career they like and to become successful. So many graduates end up regretting that they didn't take networking seriously earlier in their careers. Unfortunately, this sentiment is often uttered by the same graduates who are having trouble finding jobs. You need a network while you are still on campus.

It takes considerable effort to develop a robust network that will provide you with the resources and opportunities you'll need for your career. "The idea is to develop a network before you need it," Dan Schwabel writes in *Me 2.0: 4 Steps to Building Your Future* (2010). Taking this sound advice can spare you months of stress, frantic planning before graduation, and many hours wasted on random applications and cold-calling. Never stop networking, and more importantly, never stop diversifying your network.

4

YOUR PERSONAL BRAND

"If I take care of my character,
my reputation will take care of me."

– *Dwight L. Moody*

A *brand*, in layman's terms, is who and what people consider you to be. Essentially, it is your identity. As you continue to grow, so must your brand. College is where you spend—or *should* be spending—the most time and effort maturing and building a foundation that will result in a positive brand. Your brand is influenced by habits, rumors, conversations, relationships. The things you say and talk about, the things that you post and share online—these are the ingredients that make up your brand.

How can you mold your brand so that it works *for* you, and not *against* you? Building a strong brand involves understanding that your brand is a name tag that helps people identify who you are. Whether your brand is constantly in the forefront of your mind or not, it is always being shaped and cemented by everything you do as well as what you fail to do.

Discovering Your Brand

Having a brand requires you to "find yourself." Who are you, and how does the outside world see you? Sooner or later, you're going to have to start testing yourself.

High school students are typically concerned about what they are wearing, and whether the other kids think they're cool. As we mature, we begin to ask ourselves more philosophical questions. Where am I going in life? Am I happy with my life right now? Am I maintaining a balance between physical health and mental health, social well-being and financial well-being? Am I investing in myself versus succumbing to the external pressures of life? Does the outside world see me as someone on a path to success?

Building an Effective Brand

The answers to these probing questions are the foundations of your personal brand—your goals, dreams, opportunities. Your brand is ultimately contingent upon your ability to ask yourself these intense, deeply personal questions and come up with meaningful answers that you act upon.

Questions like these are also important because they help you discover the steps you need to take to succeed. Networking, opportunity-seeking, and relationship-building will help you understand your true interests, potential, and direction in life. Unfortunately, too many people let their brand go, either because they're too consumed with trivial pursuits and aren't truly investing in themselves or because there is something deep inside of them holding them back.

Choose Your Friends Wisely

One way to remain on the path to success is to make friends with people who are also heading that way. This doesn't mean you should drop friends who don't seem interested in professional success. It simply means that you should add to your group of close friends. Everyone needs motivation to succeed, and it can be difficult to be the only one motivating youself, especially if you're trying to get into a competitive field and are facing a lot of rejections. If all of your friends are putting their professional careers on hold so they can live leisurely, they aren't going to say the things you need to hear to stay motivated. Make friends with people who share your drive and motivation. Introduce each other to professionals who may be able to advance your careers and give each other advice on résumés and applications.

Get a Mentor

A mentor is a professional with much more experience than you who is willing to guide and teach you. I've had many mentors over the years, and today I mentor a few people myself. You're not losing out by having only one mentor; it's definitely quality over quantity. Having more than one mentor, however, has the advantage of exposing you to different philosophies and values. This will help you create your own blueprint for success.

Most colleges and universities have mentorship programs, generally through their alumni networks. Go to your campus's career services center, ask a professor in your department, or ask your boss or supervisor. There are also great programs and websites online where you can connect with mentors. The advice you receive from them can be invaluable.

Still, your mentor needn't be your boss, professor, or superior. The relationship with your mentor must feel natural; it should grow over time and shouldn't be forced. A mentor is someone who you respect and truly believe you can learn from. Unlike coaches, who develop skill sets, mentors develop people.

Role Models

Role models are not mentors, although some might turn into mentors over time. A role model could be someone who you know but don't often come into contact with, like your company's CEO. Or it could be someone you have no way of reaching at all, like an iconic figure or a celebrity. Role models are simply professionals who "model" the kind of "role" you'd like to play in life. They do not provide you with personalized feedback and advice the way a mentor does. Instead, role models can provide you with important elements of your personal blueprint for success.

Whatever you want to do in life, there are probably at least a few people who have already done it—or are doing it now. This is a good thing. Luckily, thanks to the Internet, it is easy to learn from someone you don't actually have the ability to talk to. Choose your role models carefully and learn from them by watching their interviews and documentaries online. Read their books, especially memoirs and biographies about them, and follow their stories. More importantly, try to understand what they've done, or are doing now, to succeed. What habits do they practice daily? What have they been through, and how have they overcome life's obstacles? No matter how wealthy or successful your role models are, they are still human. Find out what they've done to get there so you can start making your way there, too.

Teach Yourself How to Learn

Being an independent learner is key to shaping your brand and, ultimately, to shaping your life. Mark Zuckerberg put it very simply: "Smart people love learning." I would go as far as to say that successful people are addicted to learning.

If you're like me, you'll sometimes find yourself wrapped up in several books at a time. Of course, if you have an amazing memory, you may be able to retain everything you read, even if it's across a variety of subjects and topics. But if you are like me, then you know that method of reading only gets you an inch deep and mile wide; it rarely allows you to scratch the surface of the content. I've recently changed my reading habits because of this. I no longer read through a variety of topics and subjects throughout the year. I now attach a reading theme to each year, reading a dozen or so books on a particular topic or subject, allowing me to sharpen my focus and memory.

Just like businesses, books cater to certain markets and audiences. In order to determine if I am the audience the book is intended for, I ask myself two questions:

> *"Can I honestly comprehend this book?"*
> When I first developed the habit of reading, I always tried to challenge myself. I soon learned, however, that there is a thin line between challenging yourself and wearing yourself out. It is important to challenge yourself when learning, but the more easily something is understood, the quicker it can be ingested and applied. Reading on your

reading level is the best way to gradually improve your comprehension skills. If you find yourself lost in a book, it is not the right book for you.

"Can I readily apply this book's lessons?"
I love to read books about business and politics, but I am neither a CEO nor a politician. I've learned to read those kinds of books in moderation and instead focus on reading books with information I can readily apply. I'll invest more of my time in those books when the time is right. There's nothing wrong with reading a book for entertainment, but if you're reading to gain an idea of what to do in an area of your life, it's important to gauge how applicable the book is. For instance, if you're running for president of a club and you pick up a book on how to run for President of the United States, you won't be able to apply much of the advice. However, I have found that reading books that are not immediately applicable can help me hold my own during business or political conversations at networking events. Determine what you want to get out of reading each book, and always seek to achieve that goal.

Reading about successful people and enterprises will help you understand what you need to know to become successful. Don't view independent reading as a chore; rather, view it as a voluntary activity that will make you a better person. The most successful people are often those who read the most. If you ask any successful professional what their favorite book is, they'll have an immediate answer.

Voracious reading not only exposes you to new ideas but also improves your comprehension skills, short-term memory, vocabulary, and writing abilities. It teaches you to become more focused, and with that, present in any moment. Being fully engaged and present is a challenge for most people. If your attention always seems to be wandering when people speak, and you can't recall things that someone told you just days earlier, you will come across as scatterbrained, making people hesitate to trust you with important tasks.

As with networking, there's no such thing as too much learning. How much time do you dedicate to school, work, and those around you? How much time do you really spend investing in yourself? Many people say that they don't have time to read, but there are 168 hours in every week. More precious than money, time is something you need to learn how to budget well, because it is one thing you'll never get back. If you don't spend some time working on yourself and investing in your future, your success will be quite brief—or non-existent.

Become a Subject Matter Expert

It can be difficult to zoom in on a single career path, field or interest. And while it's great to have an intellectual appetite, employers need to know you are focused on what you're doing. Even more importantly, you can go crazy trying to focus on several career interests at once. Try to zero in on one interest at a time and direct your energy into drilling down. Learn as much as you need to know about that interest. Try to look at life through the lens of your future self. Do you want to be, say, a lawyer? Analyze every situation like a lawyer would. Treat every problem like a case and emphasize the logic and outcome of everything. Want to be a banker? Break problems into financial equations and see where you can save time and effort. Want to be a marketing or communications mogul? Delve into the psychology and behavioral patterns behind situations or problems. Observe how people act, communicate, and interact. Life must be observed from some perspective; consciously determine yours. Everyone is known for something, but no one is known for everything. After you gain a grip on a specific field of interest, use that perspective to branch out to other interests.

License Your Personal Brand

Business cards are essential for "licensing" your brand. Whether you're a junior in high school or a sophomore in college, you should have a "networking" card.

I know what you're thinking: "I haven't started my career, nor do I own a business, so why should I have a business card?" A business card places a stamp of professionalism on your brand everywhere you go and with everyone you meet.

Not surprisingly, most college students do not have a business card. If you want to stand out at networking events, it behooves you to have a business card. I can recall several times when professionals have been favorably impressed by me simply because I had a business card to share with them. You don't have to carry them with you all the time; just remember to take them with you to networking events and conferences.

Your business card only needs to contain basic contact data: your name, current city and state (leave out your street address in case you drop one in a public place), your telephone number, e-mail address, and your LinkedIn username. You can also include the name of the college or university you attend and a title—something simple like "Engineering Undergraduate."

Other ways to license your brand include starting a blog on a topic related to the field you wish to enter and/or creating a website, starting an organization on campus, or even launching your own company. Building something from scratch or doing something on your own that helps promote your skills and identity as a young professional is the best way to license and promote your brand. It is this type of activity that differentiates you in the work world and wins over employers, who are always looking for innovative, prudent, and ambitious individuals.

Travel and Explore

Traveling is not only fun, but it can also shape your brand. You can develop your brand by traveling to different conferences, taking vacations and road trips with friends, or by studying abroad. Everyone needs a change of environment once in a while as a way to click the "refresh button." Exploring the world develops your mind—people who love to explore generally have large appetites for learning and personal growth. Moreover, you should let your mind travel as much as your body. Learn about different cultures, attend events outside of your known interests, and do things that will push you out of your current comfort zone. These suggestions will expand your horizons and, in turn, you will be able to expand your comfort zone and knowledge base.

Have Meaningful Conversations

The thought processes you use to work through problems at home are often the same ones you need to solve problems at work. Everyone has personal problems, but successful people know how to deal with them in a mature manner and are careful to keep them away from the workplace. Knowing how to resolve problems by having meaningful conversations with those who are involved will make you happier in your personal life and better at work. Develop this skill, but do not breach the barriers that must exist between your personal and professional lives.

Accept Your Failures and Bad Experiences

Do not try to suppress failures or fixate on them; instead, learn from them and move on. Coping with your failures and weaknesses means objectively understanding how you felt at a given moment and why, so you know what *not* to do the next time a similar situation arises. Most importantly, always take full responsibility for your actions. Do not try to pin blame on anyone else.

Indulge in Your Good Memories

You need to remember and celebrate the genuinely happy moments in your life to get through the hard times. Thinking positively makes you so much more productive. Don't let internal tensions or tedious conflicts rob you of peace of mind. If you continue to feed the negativity in your life, you'll get less done at work, your coworkers will avoid you, and you'll be a genuinely unhappy person. At that point, it won't matter if you have your dream job.

If you're having trouble staying positive or focusing, meditation and yoga are techniques that can be very helpful—I do yoga every week, and I try to meditate as much as possible. There are many ways to meditate and countless books to instruct you on these options.

Self-Assessment

Sometimes life takes unexpected turns, forcing you to reassess your direction. At such crossroads I find it helpful to spend time prioritizing goals and interests based on their relative importance rather than on impulse and pleasure. Think about the goals you've set for yourself, your progress in achieving them, and whether they're still the goals you want to reach.

Let's say you achieved the goal of getting a job at a bank, but once you started working you realized you were unhappy there. You're not stuck at that job forever. Quitting is always an option. What is your new goal then? Where will you go after you quit the job at the bank? What do you need to do to achieve your new goal?

Don't make these kinds of life-altering decisions too hastily. In other words, don't quit simply because you had a bad day or two at work; no job is without some bad days. Evaluate where you are and compare it to where you want to be. If they match, that's great. If they don't, figure out what you need to do to change the direction of your life. The best time to look for a new job is while you still have one.

Your Digital Presence

Taking advantage of digital platforms is an essential element of brand-building in the 21st century. Here's proof: Google your name. Everything that comes up on your screen about you (or someone with the same name as yours) is something your employers can also see.

Companies employ people whose job it is to look you up when you apply for a position. In addition to what they can find on a search engine, they also cull as much information about you as possible from your Twitter, Facebook, and LinkedIn accounts, as well as any blogs or websites you contribute to. This often tells them all they want to know about you. Employers are well aware of what may go on at parties, but they need to know if you are mature enough to keep that part of your life out of the office. If you are not, it is often a deal-breaker. You will not even get an interview—no matter how marvelous your résumé is. Your "in-person brand" must align with your "digital brand."

Navigating LinkedIn

Now that you have networked to develop connections, what do you do with them? LinkedIn is a social network that helps you discover and retain professional connections as well as advertise your brand. It doesn't really matter how often you post to Facebook. LinkedIn is a platform you need to routinely update and stay active on. This is critical because a far larger number of professionals actively seek candidates for employment on LinkedIn than on Facebook. Many people consider Facebook to be a personal platform and LinkedIn to be a platform for professionals.

Where to Start?

Do not begin to add connections and share information via LinkedIn until your profile is complete. Take the time to upload your educational and professional experience, a professional photo, and a few details that will make your profile engaging. You wouldn't send an employer a draft of your cover letter or résumé, right? You would revise them first. The same is true of your LinkedIn profile.

Use this checklist to create a strong profile:

1. Professional Photo

A profile photo is critical. Potential employers and fellow professionals want to know what you look like, and by putting a face to your name, the foundation is laid for a professional relationship. Many professionals admit that they don't even bother looking at LinkedIn profiles or consider accepting a connection if the profile lacks a photo.

One myth is that you should always wear a suit or dress for your LinkedIn profile photo. Professionalism is not strictly limited to a suit and tie. There are many different types of professionals on LinkedIn. They aren't all businessmen or businesswomen, nor are they all wearing suits. One of my cousins has a nice photo of himself wearing his graduation gown. Another cousin is a nurse, so he has a photo of himself in his nursing scrubs. A professional photo is simply a respectable photo— no selfies or funny faces, please. It's easiest to look professional in a business clothes, but it's certainly not mandatory.

2. Headline

This is simply a title that identifies your professional self. If you spend time helping your peers like I do, your headline might read "Peer Consultant." If you want a job that involves writing, use "Writer." If you hold a position in a campus club or organization, include that. If you can't think of something that stands out, simply indicate your status as a student: for example, "Student at Syracuse University."

3. Industry

Be sure to list the industry you'd like to break into, being careful to use the key terms that are most likely to be searched. Watch your spelling!

4. Username/URL

This is the address of your profile: A direct link to your profile page (i.e. LinkedIn.com/in/**Louis7393**). Be sure to edit your profile username to make it easy for employers to find you. Add your link to different online platforms and be sure to include it on your résumé and business cards. Include your LinkedIn URL in your email signature also.

5. Profile Summary

Think of this as an executive summary. Summarize who you are professionally in just a few sentences. What kind of work have you done over the past few years? What are your areas of interests and expertise? What are you doing now, and what would you like to do? There's no template—and it's not a piece of cake since most college students have little to no professional experience—but you should still have goals and interests. Elaborate on those.

If, on the other hand, you're having trouble jamming a ton of experience into your summary, just exhibit your passion for a particular career path. Leverage your academic experience. Mention how your academic interests are related to the industry or field you would like to break into. Your summary shouldn't be long, and you can change it as often as you like as you gain experience and decide what your "thing" is.

Sample Profile Summary:

> I am a young professional pursuing a Bachelor of Arts in business administration with a concentration in marketing. I have a strong passion for and career interest in real estate. Although my professional experience may not yet lie in real estate, the coursework I've taken and the information I've absorbed translate well into many skills that are necessary for a career in real estate. My understanding of the many dimensions of marketing will help me attract and retain business, as well as market

efficient solutions and strategies, adding great value to any work environment.

6. Experience

Here's the piece of cake. LinkedIn allows you to directly upload your résumé from your computer to your profile. Before taking this step, make sure your résumé is up to date and error-free. After you upload, check to be sure that it was imported correctly.

7. Skills and Expertise

Include skills relevant to your experiences and interests which complement the industry you would like to break into. LinkedIn is awesome in that it allows you to include those core competencies we talked so much about in previous chapters. These go in the "Skills and Expertise" section. Keep in mind what skills and expertise employers in your industry are looking for. They don't necessarily have to be extensive or technical skills; they can be areas of interest that you are just beginning to understand.

8. Interests

Do not leave this field empty. This makes you appear boring. Just because this is a professional network does not mean you have to neglect your personal interests. Boring does *not* mean professional. Golfing, art, and entrepreneurship are some of the interests I've added to my own profile.

9. Volunteer Causes and Experience

Do not neglect this section either, even if you do not have anything specific in mind. Leaving this section empty shows employers that you are not very proactive or community conscious—two things that will hurt your brand. Studies have shown that volunteering increases your chances of employment.

Follow Step by Step

These steps are essential if you are to have a full profile. Of course, your profile may not initially appear as vibrant or as full as some of your friends who have been on LinkedIn longer. Do not allow how your profile looks at first glance to discourage you—you need to continually update and edit it anyway. After all, it is your online résumé and your résumé should be updated and edited regularly. LinkedIn also does a good job of walking you through the "get up" when you first create and edit your profile. As you build more experience on LinkedIn, you can expand your profile by filling out the sections for awards, published works, research, test scores, and more.

Be Proactive

LinkedIn is becoming more and more important to employers in the hiring process, so just about everyone has a profile. Don't run off and join one of those *"recent graduate looking for opportunities in XYZ"* groups on LinkedIn. These groups are usually saturated with thousands of recent and ready graduates competing for the same opportunities as you. The probability of securing a job opportunity through one of these groups is so low that it's not even worth joining. Instead, join groups that match your interests. The more specific you are about your interests the better. There are thousands of groups on LinkedIn, so it's all about seeing which ones fit you the best. Check the level of activity and what kinds of professionals are in the group. Groups that are rarely active are *dead groups*.

Idleness is not an option on LinkedIn. If you're not going to actively participate in a group you're better off not joining it at all. Express your presence and interest by "liking" articles, posting comments, and participating in discussions. Professionals like to share their thoughts and experiences on LinkedIn. They also like to keep abreast of their endorsers and supporters, so "liking" their articles serves as a good introduction before you ask to connect. It also shows employers that you are genuinely interested. The e-mail notifications can get annoying, but you can easily control the pace at which you receive them by adjusting your settings.

The discussions you start on LinkedIn should be productive also. Again, it's like regular networking. Post discussions or questions about current trends in your industry. Exchange ideas and thoughts, and start making new connections. It's not possible to actively participate in dozens of groups at the same time, so you'll find yourself leaving and joining many groups as your interests migrate and develop. Be sure to leave groups that you are not actively involved in. How do you expect to build connections if you're not even aware of them?

Make Searching People a Habit

This is probably the single most important activity to practice. The only way to take full advantage of LinkedIn is by—of course—connecting with people! Make it a habit to search for people on LinkedIn: your friends, professors, professionals, alumni, faculty, and the people you've met recently while networking. As you become active on LinkedIn, this practice will move to the forefront of your brain. I suggest that you *do not* accept or add people who you do not know and have never met personally. Some people are *open connectors*; they connect with anyone and everyone for no apparent reason. If someone randomly sends a connection request, browse their profile to see if you share any connections. If you are interested in connecting, see if they share any mutual interests and skills. Maybe they currently or previously worked at a company you're interested in. This can indicate if a *productive relationship* is possible. Do not accept or send a connection request unless you have introduced yourself and explained why you are interested in connecting with them. Connect with a purpose.

Don't be afraid to surf through profiles and introduce yourself. That is exactly how you expand your network. Your network is made up of first-, second-, and third-degree connections—second- and third-degree connections being people with whom you share mutual connections. The more people you directly connect with, the more people you'll have in your network, and more connections can lead to new jobs and opportunities.

Stay in the Know

Sharing and posting articles regularly on LinkedIn will bolster your brand and help you secure opportunities. Share news and articles about the latest trends and biggest players in your industry. Who's doing what and who's saying what about whom? Share things you find personally interesting, and share jobs or opportunities you may have come across but are not interested in to help others in your network as well.

Follow Companies, Influencers, Groups and Hashtags

LinkedIn makes breaking into the workforce even easier by allowing you to virtually visit the companies you may be interested in working for. Follow key companies to receive news about job postings and internship opportunities in your area. Moreover, LinkedIn shows you how many of your connections are affiliated with that company. Knowing who will be able to introduce you to "strategic others" is imperative. Know who your resources are.

Be sure to also follow people who LinkedIn refers to as *Influencers*: LinkedIn professionals who regularly share great content with enormous audiences that are usually in the tens of thousands. These people are the greatest information hubs on LinkedIn, so being affiliated with them and being active in their discussions is crucial to building an influential brand and making connections.

You also need to follow hashtags. Formerly, LinkedIn used a different grouping mechanism, so any member could share articles on a specific topic in a specific place and reach people interested in that topic. Now LinkedIn has followed other social media sites in using hashtags. You can write a post from your home page, hashtag it with the most appropriate subject and it will appear in the hub for that hashtag. If it gains popularity, it may also appear in the news feeds of those following that hashtag. Examples of hashtags you can follow are: #personalbranding, #leadershipdevelopment, and #strategicthinking. There is a hashtag for just about everything, so follow the ones most relevant to your field and the topics you'd like to learn more about and potentially connect with people to discuss.

Endorse Connections

LinkedIn also lets people endorse each other's qualifications. A person who knows you possess a skill you've listed on your profile can endorse that skill on your profile, showing employers that you truly do have the skills you've listed. This can reflect well on you, but it also has the unfortunate effect of causing people to make negative assumptions about users with few or no endorsements.

People will naturally endorse you for skills they see you demonstrating, and be sure to endorse others so that they can return the favor. Remember that LinkedIn is your professional online presence. People like to browse and search profiles, so the more profiles you are on the better. Start endorsing people!

Write and Ask for Recommendations

Recommendations, of course, help to build a positive image around your brand. Employers and professionals like to know that people are confident in your abilities and therefore in your brand. Receiving recommendations shows credibility, but providing others with recommendations does that too— if not more. Recommending people on LinkedIn shows you are a leader and that you have the experience you claim to have, while helping you nurture and build relationships with existing connections.

I have a technique I use to stay proactive on LinkedIn; I call it the *LinkedIn Ratio*. For every person who recommends me, I make sure to recommend at least two existing connections. I recommend friends, of course, and the professionals that I meet. I've written recommendations for the professionals I've met at large speaking events and book signings. Expect to build firm relationships with professionals you meet at networking events and conferences if you take the time to recognize their accomplishments and experiences. A recommendation does not have to be lengthy, just a short paragraph that summarizes their skills and expertise, including your relationship and experience with the connection.

How to Find a Job on LinkedIn

You'll regularly get job suggestions and e-mail notifications from LinkedIn regarding opportunities that match your profile, but you can also take a proactive approach and seek jobs yourself on LinkedIn. Simply look for a tab on the home page that reads *Jobs* and use the search box to look for jobs in a particular field—law, finance, marketing, accounting, etc.

It's necessary to stay active and update your LinkedIn profile regularly because as you continue to add to your profile, share news, and build connections, LinkedIn will generate more and more jobs tailored to your needs and profile. Jobs are usually sorted by the most recent posting date, giving you time to reach out to professionals and tailor your résumé for each job before applications close.

Connecting with Alumni

Finding and connecting with alumni couldn't be easier on LinkedIn. This is a great advantage because your school's alumni are the largest network of professionals available to connect you with opportunities, help you build a network, and further develop your professional brand. Alumni are usually very excited to help people from their alma mater. I've reached out to and connected with many alumni for professional opportunities, advice, and mentorship. The alumni search engine allows you to target a specific audience, and you can zoom in as much as you wish. Search for alumni by location, occupation, company, degree, graduation class, skills, and other filters. If you're looking to get into accounting, for example, search for alumni who recently graduated and are now in accounting positions. If you're curious about what opportunities your degree can lead to, look for alumni who studied what you're studying now. Mix and exclude search categories to generate successful searches that address your unique needs.

If you're simply interested in building a solid network and seeking mentors, contacting alumni is a great place to start. Remember to be courteous and mindful of their time. Here is an e-mail example of how to approach an alumnus on LinkedIn:

Greetings Joe,

I hope you don't mind my reaching out, but I am a junior at XYZ University. I noticed that you studied marketing during your undergraduate career, and I am eager to learn more about the marketing world and the opportunities it has to offer. If you happen to have time in your schedule, I'd love to speak with you on the phone or perhaps take you out for coffee. I look forward to hearing from you. Thank you.

Sincerely,

[Your name]

Keep Track of Your Activity

Visibility will help you the most in finding and making connections on LinkedIn. Keeping track of your activity is extremely important because it will help you understand your progress and recognize if there are ways you can improve your profile. LinkedIn regularly delivers statistics about your network, activity, and industry. You can check who and how many people have been visiting your profile, as well as keywords that have led them to you. Keywords are important everywhere, especially on LinkedIn. You can also see how many views you've received on things you have posted and shared, and suggestions for pages, groups, and people you may know.

Join LinkedIn!

Becoming involved in LinkedIn doesn't take a lot of time. I understand that LinkedIn may seem a little boring in the beginning, but it isn't solely geared toward experienced professionals looking to climb their respective corporate ladders. Becoming active on LinkedIn will help you get a head start, whether you're a freshman or a senior. Think of it like this: it's just one place you go to run all your "professional errands." This is where you network, share and read news about your industry and interests, prepare for interviews, get advice and mentorship, find jobs, and more. All the things you need to pursue your career goals, all in one place. Isn't that convenient?

Digital Presence, Continued

A weak online presence can hurt you in certain situations depending on what field you're trying to enter. Many key players in the media industry look for candidates who generate high online traffic and influence cyberspace in some capacity, whether through a blog, website, or app. Some positions I've applied to in marketing and communications asked me how many followers I have on Twitter and how many friends I have on Facebook. Online presence holds a large stock in some industries—usually industries that thrive online.

The biggest use of my own online presence is *reverse networking*. I mostly use my social media to recognize other people and relay opportunities. I tweet and tag people's accomplishments and current endeavors, and I give people kudos. I make sure that my online presence serves to add great positivity to my environment. How much of your time do you spend online congratulating yourself versus your friends?

Offensive and Defensive Branding

Offensive and *defensive branding* are sets of strategies employed to manage and promote your image. Whether you're aware of it or not, you're promoting and defending your brand daily. The only way to improve your brand is by being aware of what effects certain habits, hobbies, and personal appearances have on your brand.

Offensive branding involves tactics that directly promote your brand; taking the initiative to start a club or creating a blog are examples of *offensive branding*. Alternatively, *defensive branding* refers to tactics used to further emphasize your existing brand. For example: I'm someone who likes to dress well, and I believe that the way that I dress—casual blazers, button downs, and wingtip shoes—complements my brand. When people began to say that I always looked professional, I made it a habit to dress that way more often. I'm also known to have a book or newspaper in hand. When people commented on that habit as well, I realized that merely walking around with the *Wall Street Journal* helped complement my professional attire, and thus, my brand. Of course, I genuinely appreciate reading and I dress business casual because that's my style, but because I am conscious of how these habits influence my brand, I can take advantage of them.

These branding tactics allow me to take control of my brand, and in the process, help me become a better me. Small habits and appearances act as great branding tactics. Take notice of what you're doing right, and then try to do it more often or even better. For instance, I asked myself, "How can I make reading and self-development reflect my brand *more*?" Now, when I'm in town visiting a friend, I occasionally bring them a book as a gift. Of course, I genuinely care about the success of my friends, but I do it more often than before because I understand the influence it has on my brand—even if they don't. Think of yourself as a major corporate brand. Companies spend countless hours and dollars building, defending, and promoting their brands, as well as keeping an eye on brand consistency.

Authenticity and consistency are the core ideas behind brand management. Offensive and defensive branding are most effective when you are conscious of how certain habits, appearances, and hobbies are perceived by others. It's all about taking control and making these everyday things work *for* you and not against you. Once you understand brand management, you can begin strategizing and thinking of new ways to promote your brand.

What Does Your Brand Say?

If you don't take control of your brand, the people around you will. Consciously take matters into your own hands and remain aware and in control of how the outside world perceives you. Why? Because the outside world includes those same professionals, professors, and connections who decide whether you get the job or not, or whether you deserve that scholarship or not, or whether you're going to get into that program or not. Your brand is a generator that can never—ever—be turned off. Your posts online, conversations you had weeks ago with friends and family, personal habits and hobbies, relationships, conflicts, and problems—they ALL influence your brand.

5

E-MAIL ETIQUETTE

*"The single biggest problem in communication
is the illusion that it has taken place."*

– George Bernard Shaw

The purpose of an e-mail is very simple: it is a call for action. As you make your way into the professional world, you will begin using e-mail more than any other medium. People, especially experienced professionals, will often organize their day as dictated by their inboxes. They plan, schedule, and prioritize meetings and tasks according to the e-mails they send and receive. Therefore, it is especially important to understand that e-mail communication is only necessary when action is required. If a task requires extensive thought or further communication, you're better off calling or scheduling an appointment. When writing an e-mail, you need to ask yourself: what is it that needs to be done, and who is the right person to speak to about it?

The Shorter, the Better

When you're writing an e-mail, think in terms of tweeting: keep it short and concise. That is the number one rule of e-mail composition. Often people send e-mails that are too long, and things wind up not getting done. Lengthy e-mails are often tossed aside to be read later and are eventually forgotten. Shorter e-mails allow people to organize their thoughts easily and act upon their response, as opposed to wasting time trying to process the longer e-mail. Your e-mail should get straight to the point and provide the recipient with a clear understanding of what needs to be done.

Think Forward

Forward thinking is a must in e-mail writing. You are, after all, calling for future action, so why not aim to answer any and all questions that might arise? Put yourself in your recipient's shoes. After reading this e-mail, would you have any follow-up questions? Would you truly understand what needs to be done? Include any information or suggestions that will help facilitate communication. Include important dates, attachments, or references that will ease the process.

Cut Out the Fat

I've read too many e-mails that include so much unnecessary information that by the time I've finished reading them, I've lost the point. I'm mentally exhausted and simply cannot respond. You need to cut out the fat. Re-reading e-mails before you send them out is not only important for grammatical clarity and proper spelling but also for checking for any passages that are repetitive or unnecessary to convey your main point. Moreover, longer e-mails are as exhausting for the sender as they are for the recipient and increase the risk of making grammatical errors. Every sentence must be pertinent and succinct! If you find yourself writing a long e-mail, there are a few things you can do to cut down the length:

- **Bullets/Lists.** These are most helpful because they help not only to paraphrase but also to organize ideas and thoughts, so your reader won't have to.

- **Move to another medium.** If you notice an e-mail conversation is dragging on too long, suggest handling business in person or over the phone.

The Subject

A subject is not a sentence. Do not make it more than a few words. I only use special characters such as commas, colons, and semicolons when I want to separate important information in a subject line (e.g. Job Application: Summer Analyst 2018, ID: 47388832). Utilizing special characters versus conjunctions such as "and, or, etc.," saves space and helps keep your subject short and concise. Do not use all caps to write your subject line, even if it's an urgent message. People naturally read all caps as shouting, and shouting at your coworkers—even via e-mail and even if you didn't intend to—is unprofessional. The subject should simply be a phrase that captures the gist of the e-mail as well as your recipient's attention. If possible, it should insinuate some call to action.

The Power of Courteous Language

Re-read your e-mail and put yourself in the recipient's shoes. What is the tone of the e-mail? Even without intending to—just as with a sarcastic tone of voice or blank facial expression—a poorly written e-mail can turn off a recruiter or professional. You must be able to understand how your writing may be interpreted. You want to appear as respectful and humble in your writing as possible, and you should be able to do it without using emoticons or acronyms like "lol," which are very unprofessional. When you re-read your e-mails, make sure your intentions are clear.

For example, say you've sent a document to a coworker for review and are waiting for her to return it so you can continue with the task you need to perform. Sending an e-mail to follow up after a reasonable amount of time has passed is acceptable, but if you just write "Did you look at that document yet?" your coworker may sense hostility in that one line and become angry or defensive. Although shorter is better, you don't want to make it too short to convey the appropriate tone. A better e-mail would read something like:

Hi, [Coworker's name],

I just wanted to follow up with you regarding that document. Would it be possible for you to return it after lunch, or will you need more time with it?

This e-mail is longer but more respectful and harder to interpret as hostile. Still, such miscommunications are why you're sometimes better off picking up the phone or stopping by someone's desk if possible.

E-mail Tone

The key to writing professional e-mails is to match your tone to that of the person with whom you're corresponding. If you've corresponded with the recipient before, look at the way he or she writes and match your tone to that. If she's very brusque and to the point, don't ramble. If he wishes you a good morning and asks how your weekend was, respond in a similar manner. If you're writing to a person you've never corresponded with before, err on the side of formality. Keep it short and sweet, free of emoticons and personal questions.

When to Use CC and BCC

CC (carbon copy), and *BCC* (blind carbon copy), are e-mail features that allow you to include several recipients in your e-mail. Sometimes e-mail conversations involve an exchange between more than two parties. You're going to need to know who else to include and where to include them in the conversation.

Carbon Copies

Obviously, your main point of contact is the recipient to whom you'll be sending the e-mail directly. This is the person who will probably be leading the action, while the CC'ed addressees are the people who are, or will be, involved with the conversation (e.g. someone's assistant or colleague). Including those other team members is one of those forward-thinking actions you employ which will help facilitate the communication process. When you copy someone to an e-mail, or when you are communicating with two or more people in the same e-mail, address each person appropriately. For example, say you're coordinating a group project:

Greetings,

I hope this e-mail finds you all well. As discussed, we will be meeting on Friday to complete the business project. I have outlined and addressed everyone's role accordingly and have copied all the necessary parties. Please feel free to copy and address any party you feel is missing from the e-mail exchange. Thank you.

Jessica: We should finish the analysis on Company C by Thursday. If you can include the actual and estimated budget, it would be much appreciated.

Harvey: How is the table looking for Company B's framework? Please update us with your progress up until this point, including any and all questions or concerns you may have.

Mike: Let's sit down individually since we are both working on Company A's evaluation. If possible, let's do Thursday at 2 p.m.?

I'm very proud of the progress we are making and believe we are on a great track. If I have missed anything, please address it and copy all parties.

Best,

In this example, I used colons and sub-paragraphs to separate information so that it reads smoothly. I was courteous yet concise in my language, and I also laid out all the necessary information, dates, etc. Sending this one e-mail to all three people lets everyone working on the project see what needs to be done and saves me from having to manage three separate e-mail conversations.

Blind Carbon Copies

These are less common than carbon copies. Blind carbon copy is an e-mail feature that camouflages addressees—the e-mail address is only visible to the sender. Any BCC'ed recipient will not be seen by the primary recipient, though the BCC'ed recipients will be able to see the primary recipient. Use BCC to send a mass e-mail to many people who do not know one another. E-mail etiquette requires that you do not make people's personal e-mail addresses public to others without their consent or knowledge. For example, if you needed to send the same e-mail to twelve different clients, none of whom know each other, you could use BCC to save yourself from having to send the same e-mail twelve different times, while keeping everyone's e-mail addresses private.

Check Your E-mail for the Three "C"s

Concise: Remember—the shorter, the better. Read it over to see if there are any unnecessary sentences. Also, check for run-on sentences or any redundancies. Remember to use bullets or semicolons when necessary!

Clarity: Think forward when writing your e-mail. What follow-up questions, if any, might your recipient(s) have? Be sure to address them in advance. Is the call for action obvious or do you need to be clearer? Have you facilitated the communication process by laying out all the necessary information in the e-mail (e.g. dates, ideas, numbers, references, links)? Is there anything you can say that would provide further clarification? Read the e-mail like your recipient would. Cut out the fat and keep it action-oriented.

Courteous: Try to be very respectful and welcoming with your language. Use polite language, such as, "Please and thank you," "If possible," and "I hope it is not a bother but..." Again, read the e-mail like your recipient would. How does the tone come across to you?

Managing Your E-Mail

I never open an e-mail unless I plan to respond to it at that moment. People have a habit of opening their e-mails and then forgetting to respond after they leave them open. Always reserve time during the day to check and respond to e-mail. Also make sure to check your e-mail every day. Perhaps your personal life doesn't require you to check your e-mail each day, but in the workplace it's imperative that you do so. Learn and understand e-mail etiquette now because you're going to be playing catch-up if you don't.

6

LEADERSHIP

"Our deepest fear is not that we are inadequate.
Our deepest fear is that we are powerful beyond measure.
It is our light, not our darkness, that most frightens us."

– *Marianne Williamson*

How do you inspire yourself? When I was sixteen or seventeen, I began to devour self-help literature—the best books and documentaries about success and life I could find. I read *From Good to Great* by Jim Collins, *The Secret* by Rhonda Byrne, and *How to Win Friends and Influence People* by Dale Carnegie. The book that changed my life, though, was *Think and Grow Rich* by Napoleon Hill.

That book ignited something amazing in me. It also taught me two truths: 1) your success is determined by your self-worth, and 2) desire equals discipline. I desired success more than anything, so I became disciplined and determined. Soon, the two or three books I was reading each week weren't enough.

I started absorbing the biographies and stories of my greatest role models: Tony Robbins, Warren Buffet, Oprah Winfrey, Richard Branson, and Jay-Z, to name a few. I began diving deeper, searching into the lives of some of history's greatest game changers, like Aristotle, Albert Einstein, Benjamin Franklin, Henry Ford, David Rockefeller, and Thomas Edison. I watched interviews, read articles, and tried to understand their legacies.

It was about this same time that I started learning and practicing everything I have written about in this book: interviewing, résumé writing, job searching, networking, etc. I was looking for inspiration, while my subconscious was looking for answers. I began to wonder how the people I was reading about had become so successful. Through my reading and research, I was able to identify the habits that these iconic figures—generations apart—shared and embraced, and I learned how to inspire myself.

Leadership is a Journey

Put simply, being a leader means:

- Motivating and inspiring others to a purpose or shared vision

- Creating an atmosphere or space where people feel comfortable and significant

- Taking responsibility for failure or failed expectations

- Catering to the developmental and emotional needs of others

You're not going to develop leadership skills just by reading about them—you must take the initiative and follow through. You must CONSCIOUSLY lead. I urge you to take up leadership positions at school, home, and in your community. Just because you can't write a particular experience on your résumé doesn't mean it's not valuable. Even if you just want to be a better leader to your nephew by serving as a mentor, do it.

A manager has a different focus than a leader but not necessarily an opposite focus. I want to first dispel the idea that being a leader is better than being a manager. The word "manager" has developed a bad reputation as modern work norms have begun to transform. The working world is moving into an era of social leadership and open-minded work cultures, especially in corporate America. The typical, stringent, results-focused, people-pushing image of a manager just doesn't belong in the modern workplace. People don't want to be managed; they want to be led.

So, what can we do as young leaders and managers? We can redefine what it means to be a manager and a leader. Being a good manager is the yang to any leader's yin. In any situation, people are often better at one role than the other—either you're a better leader than you are a manager or vice versa—but understand that you don't give up one for the other. A manager must provide instruction. Being a manager of people was probably one of the hardest things for me to master since I wasn't comfortable with staying on top of people because I loathed the idea of being a micro-manager. I had trouble running effective meetings and creating fine lines of communication during my student organization meetings. I had to learn and learn fast.

Managership is a Process

Put simply, being a manager means:

- Creating an effective and resourceful plan of action

- Aligning appropriate resources with the respective goals

- Guiding people procedurally, step by step, to achieve a goal

- Ensuring people are on track to reach their goals

- Evaluating the process and its results, and providing constructive feedback

We are Everyday Leaders and Managers

Try to take these business concepts out of the context of your career for just a moment. Every day, even for a few seconds, you are a manager to **someone**. Being a good manager is about providing proper procedural guidance and instruction regarding a specific process or goal. When you think of a manager, think of process and procedure. Do you do that at some point in your day—even for yourself?

You have to make self-empowerment and motivation habits, but self-empowerment and motivation alone are not enough; you must also be a good manager of yourself. I had a lot of drive but not much focus while growing up. I needed to commit to my goals and promises, so that's what I learned to do, and I encourage you to learn to manage yourself as well. Go out and buy a journal and, just like with any class or exam, take notes:

study, highlight, and annotate the things you read and plan for in your personal life.

Writing things down allows you to retain and evaluate information a thousand times more effectively. When I began my independent learning and reading, I wish I had written and organized more notes. It is easier than you think to look around in your life and notice where you can be a better manager. Want to save money for vacation? Write it down, and make a plan. Write down your vision, the steps and resources necessary to satisfy your plan, and create milestones. Being a good manager depends heavily on how you utilize your resources (anything that will allow you to follow through with your plan is a resource) and organize yourself. Make sure you're working at a pace suitable to the resources you have available, and monitor progress regularly, as resource availability may change.

Remember how in earlier chapters I laid out the process of finding a job and nailing interviews? Well, the same managerial process applies to everything else in life: Write your process down, identify your resources, check in with each step, always do your research, and work your plan. Also, continually assess the results and give yourself feedback! A good manager is constantly trying to improve and repeat a good process. Can the way you study improve? What about the way you exercise? How about your diet? More importantly, how about the way you solve problems and deal with stress? These are trick questions: there is ALWAYS room for improvement in our daily lives. Your job as a good manager to find ways to continually bring effectiveness to the many different processes in your personal life.

Good Followership

One of the hardest things about being a natural leader is that it is typically hard for one *not* to lead—it's instinct. Many leaders don't realize that being a good follower will allow them to develop great leadership skills. Now, I don't mean 'follower' from a literal perspective, but from a humble one; you should learn how to appreciate and embrace the leadership of others. Learning how to be a follower teaches great humility—one of the single most important traits in a leader.

Moreover, by understanding what it means to be a subordinate, you will better understand what makes a good or bad leader. It allows you to empathize with co-workers and teaches you what mistakes not to make. It also gives you the opportunity to effectively communicate ideas and feedback to a superior. The most important thing you can do is to be honest and real with the leaders you interact with, but remember that criticizing them behind their back, or in front of their face, is just negative energy and bad politics. People often forget that managers still need honest and well-delivered feedback to improve—in fact, they need it more than anyone else. If you find that your work culture is one that does not encourage open dialogue with leadership, then I encourage you to leave.

7

THINK DIFFERENTLY

"The two most important days in our lives
are the day we are born and the day we find out why."

– Mark Twain

This book, so far, has addressed the nuances which can set you apart from others—such as your personal brand, a well-executed résumé and cover letter, stellar interview etiquette, and impressive leadership skills. These are the "Intern Talk" essentials; the perfect starter kit for any young ambitious professional. I want to emphasize that this book really isn't just for the business student, and it isn't just focused on the office intern. Whether you'd like to start your own business, go to medical school, or chase your music ambitions, everyone needs to learn these valuable lessons.

I know why you picked up this book. You picked it up because you believe in yourself. You believe that you deserve to be successful. You are confident, even though you're still building self-esteem like everyone else, and you are ambitious. You don't know where you're going in life, but you do know you're on your way.

I know who you are.

Steve Jobs once said that the crazy people are usually the ones who are crazy enough to change things—they think differently. In these final paragraphs, I want to urge you to think differently.

These are the concepts and principles I believe in and practice. They are personal, somewhat abstract, but they are what the "crazy people" have adopted—the Steve Jobs, Oprahs, Aristotles, Ralph Laurens—people who have changed things. The truth is, we know exactly what it takes to be successful, but we usually cheat ourselves out of it. One of the chief differences between those who are successful and climbing, and those who are failing and drowning, is philosophy.

The Philosophy of Success

There are too many books, documentaries, articles, and findings that talk about success for us to be ignorant about what it takes to achieve our goals. Success is really just a balance between wealth and happiness. To delve a bit more deeply, success is a system of habits that results in consistent happiness and wealth. Let's start with wealth. Power is honestly the greatest form of wealth. The Oprahs, the Steve Jobs, and the Will Smiths have all learned to liquidize and leverage that power: not necessarily a position or title, but the power of positive energy, discipline, and self-esteem. That energy we talked about earlier—the Law of Attraction—that kind of power is what it takes.

When you learn how to inspire confidence in yourself and others; when you learn how to lead versus react; when you learn to focus and invest in what you love, and not worry about anyone or anything else; when you learn to turn negative energy into positive energy—that's the greatest wealth. Do it every single day. The energy you put into studying every day or the energy you put into getting a promotion is the same energy. It's the self-empowerment—the belief you've invested into your work—that will enable you to achieve the results you've aimed for.

Finding Purpose

Mark Twain said the two most important days in your life are the day you are born, and the day you find out why. Finding your life's purpose is not about getting the right answer; it's about asking yourself the right questions to find a deeper and more interconnected purpose in your hobbies and interests. Asking questions is a skill that you need to practice, and once it becomes a habit, the gates to learning and succeeding will swing open.

Remember: live with purpose. You might not find your purpose today or tomorrow. In fact, you're probably struggling over what that purpose is right now. But the struggle itself is a good thing and will help you to eventually understand your purpose. When you begin living for a conscious and grounded purpose, you start to work and learn with purpose as well—everything becomes focused and calculated, even the most ambiguous and abstract of goals and ideas.

The struggles we see people go through every day are good and bad habits fighting for dominance. You have to learn how to look at those habits objectively without criticizing others or yourself.

Finding a habit group—a circle of friends or connections that follow similar good habits—will help to push you towards your planned goal. Whether it's weight loss, reading a new book, or working on a new idea, finding similar-minded people with healthy habit systems will aid you in finding and developing purpose.

Nothing Is Permanent

People tend not to stay focused or invested in the present and instead dwell on the past or dream about the future. Looking towards the past can create a sense of certainty for some, and we commonly scrutinize our past to retrospectively correct ourselves and our mistakes—hindsight is 20/20, of course. However, the past is what has already happened, and there is no way of going back. Did you make a mistake at work? Oh well, it happens all the time. One thing we need to remember is that nothing is permanent. Our failures or mistakes do not define us. I'm not telling you to ignore the past, but there is a difference between attempting to recreate a reality that has expired and objectively trying to understand and evaluate a past experience for its present value. From now on, you're going to have to focus on the latter.

I believe that living for the future can be even more dangerous because we all know nothing goes as planned. The danger of focusing too much on or too far into the future is that we lose our balance in the present moment. Imagine yourself balancing on a tight rope a thousand feet above ground. The future is way ahead, and you're afraid that you'll fall before you get there. Focus too far ahead and you'll lose your balance. Look back and you'll trip and fall—or you won't move forward at all. The only way to get to the end of the tight rope is to focus on each and every step you take WHILE you take it. That is what being present and conscious means.

Even if you are still struggling to decide on a career path, lean toward your strengths. Too many people try to do everything at once, or they compare themselves to friends and peers and drown under jealousy and doubt. Take calculated risks, cherish small wins, and take every failure and mistake as a lesson learned.

PARTING THOUGHTS

Your career should be a marriage between your passion and your skills. It is something that will take up most of your time and determine what kind of life you'll live and whom you'll live it with. Your career shouldn't merely be a source of money—it should be a source of happiness and purpose. You must decide that things will work out, even if they don't seem like they will at the moment. Take pride in yourself, love yourself for who you are, welcome change, and challenge life. The person you are becoming is defined by what you do every day. Stay passionate, stay focused, and stay in control.

ACKNOWLEDGMENTS

First and foremost, I'd like to thank my loving mother and father. None of this would have been possible without them. My parents are immigrants from Haiti—one a taxi driver and the other an in-home medical aide. It took an extraordinary amount of kindness, awareness, and patience to arrive in the "land of opportunity" and to raise children in a new world they knew very little about. Nonetheless, they were able to instill in me values that have allowed me to grow into the young professional I am today. That is no small feat. Everything that I am—and all of what I am looking to accomplish in life—are the result of their love and hard work.

Thanks also to the rest of my family and dear friends. No man truly travels alone. He has his thoughts and good memories to keep him sane. And it's the thoughts of dear friends and loved ones that help him find himself and his purpose. In the midst of changing the world, I ultimately hope to change your lives for the better, too.

Special thanks to Martha Gorman and the rest of my excellent publishing team. There would be no *Intern Talk* without your investment, support, and belief.

ABOUT THE AUTHOR

Anthony Louis began his career trek as an advisor to peers, providing internship consultation and inter-view coaching to hundreds of college students. Now flexing his entrepreneurial muscles in the heady start-  up world, the Brooklyn native acts as an organizational consultant to start-up founders and business leaders alike. After much success, he hopes that *Intern Talk* serves as a career beacon for aspiring young professionals.